WOMEN IN IBERIAN EXPANSION OVERSEAS
1415-1815

Luso-Brazilian ladies by Carlos Julião, *c.* 1785.
Reproduced by permission of the Biblioteca Nacional, Rio de Janeiro.

WOMEN IN IBERIAN EXPANSION OVERSEAS, 1415–1815

Some facts, fancies and personalities

C. R. Boxer

NEW YORK
OXFORD UNIVERSITY PRESS
1975

ISBN 0 19 519817 4

Printed in Great Britain by
Ebenezer Baylis and Son Limited
The Trinity Press, Worcester, and London

Library of Congress Catalog Card Number 74–32645

CONTENTS

ACKNOWLEDGMENTS

I have to thank President Wofford and the Faculty members of the Department of History for inviting me to give the Mary Flexner Lectures at Bryn Mawr College in October–November 1972, and for making my stay there so pleasant. I should add that the choice of the subject was mine alone.

I am also indebted to my friends and colleagues, Ursula Lamb of Yale University, and James Cummins of the Department of Spanish, University College, University of London, for some valuable references (not all of which I was able to use) and for the loan of books; and to Senhor Luís Gonzaga of Macao, for his help in the local archives. Last but not least, I have to thank Yale University for two travel grants which enabled me to work in the archives of the Azores in 1970 and 1972.

Similarly, I am glad to acknowledge my obligation to the Librarian and staff of the Lilly Library, Indiana University, and particularly Miss Mayellen Bresie, Curator of the Mendel Collection, for facilitating my consultation of the very rare Mexican seventeenth-century works concerning *La China Poblana*.

INTRODUCTION

As James Lockhart has observed in a perceptive and stimulating essay on the social history of colonial Spanish America, 'Women are not only an essential part of any balanced treatment of social history, but through their presence or absence, their marriages, dowries, activities, and property-owning, are an absolutely indispensable measure of the quality and velocity of general social development, as well as of any individual male's rank, prosperity, and affiliation. Women appear regularly in all the Iberian sources from cedularies to litigation; career skeletons and even full, intimate portraits are not much harder to produce for women than for men of the corresponding categories.'[1] Lockhart has shown what can be done in this respect by his brilliant exploitation of the notarial records of colonial Peru, but I cannot think of any other equally satisfying treatment of the place of women in colonial Iberian society.[2] Many of the standard works do not even have an entry for 'women' in their indices; and if women are mentioned at all, such mention is usually restricted to famous characters such as Hernando Cortéz's celebrated mistress, interpreter, and adviser in the conquest of Mexico, 'La Malinche'. I have not had the opportunity for archival research in depth on the topic which I have rashly chosen; but I hope to give some indication of the research possibilities in this field and to recall some historical figures who may be unfamiliar. It is obviously impossible to deal adequately with the subject in both range and depth in the strictly limited scope of four lectures. The treatment is therefore both episodic and severely selective, some aspects receiving only scant notice and many others being omitted altogether. Thus, in the first lecture there will be something about Iberian women in the Portuguese *praças* of Morocco, in West Africa, and in the Azores, but nothing about them in the Canaries, in the Cape Verde Islands, and in the Spanish *presidios* of North Africa. In the second lecture, there will be something about Iberian women in Mexico, Peru, and Brazil, but only passing

[1] 'The social history of colonial Spanish America', in *Latin-American Research Review*, VII, Nr. 1 (Austin, Texas, 1972), pp. 39–40.

[2] *Spanish Peru. A Colonial Society* (University of Wisconsin Press, Madison, 1968), pp. 150–70.

9

mention of them in the Caribbean Islands, and nothing about them in Venezuela or in Columbia. Similarly, their presence in some regions of Asia—where, however, they were very thin on the ground —has to be unavoidably ignored in the third lecture.

Since the published documentation on women in the Iberian colonial world is sufficient neither in quantity nor in quality to provide adequate material for 'structures', 'models', and other fashionable inter-disciplinary paraphernalia, this tentative essay does not presume to be anything more than what is explicitly indicated in the sub-title, together with some suggestions for possible future research. It has no theoretical framework and does not draw any hard and fast conclusions; but it does contain some unfamiliar material which may interest a wider circle than the audiences at Bryn Mawr which gave me such a courteous hearing.

Finally, it should be explained that the third chapter is double the original lecture length, mainly due to the special attention which I have devoted to the late Dr. Germano da Silva Correia's extremely useful, but in some respects very misleading, six-volume work on Portuguese colonisation in India.

CHAPTER ONE

Morocco, West Africa, and the Atlantic Islands

Whether Portuguese (or any other) women accompanied the expeditionary force which sailed from the Tagus in July 1415 for the capture and occupation of Ceuta, I do not know. If they did, they were presumably camp-followers rather than housewives. In any event, this episode is usually taken as marking the beginnings of Portuguese expansion overseas, which from then onwards proceeded almost uninterruptedly for nearly four centuries in one or another region of the globe. Once the decision was taken to hold Ceuta permanently, Portuguese women, or some of them, accompanied their menfolk there, and the same occurred with the other coastal strongholds that were successively conquered from the Moors in the next hundred years. With the discovery, or rediscovery, of Madeira and the Azores in *c.* 1419–50, these uninhabited Atlantic island groups were successively colonised. By the end of the fifteenth century, the Portuguese voyages of discovery and of trade (chiefly for gold, slaves and ivory) down the West African coast had provoked an annual emigration of Portuguese men, albeit of very few women, to the coastal *foci* of the gold and slave trades, to the (hitherto uninhabited) Cape Verde Islands and to São Tomé and Príncipe in the Gulf of Guinea. Promising contacts had also been made with the kingdom of Congo by the time that Columbus sailed on his famous voyage of discovery in 1492.

With the discovery and exploitation of the Cape Route to India, the volume and rate of emigration spectacularly increased in the first half of the sixteenth century, receiving a further spurt in the second half with the development of the colonisation of Brazil. By the year 1600, there were Portuguese settlers, traders, fishers and transients to be found around the world from Newfoundland to Chile, from Brazil to Japan, from Morocco to the Moluccas. These emigrants, whether temporary or permanent, came from a population which probably oscillated at something between a million and a million and a quarter souls for most of the fifteenth and sixteenth centuries. The overwhelming majority of those who left Portugal were able-bodied men, but appreciable, if still small, numbers of women went to some places, and many more were naturally born there. I will briefly consider some of these pioneer Portuguese women overseas, but I have not sufficient time or knowledge to deal with their Spanish sisters in the Canary Islands and the North African *presidios*.

The first point to stress is the almost total lack of any reliable statistics over any considerable period of time, and for many places and for many years we have no figures at all.[1] Quantitative history in this field is thus impossible, and we have to rely on a variety of sources of very different scope and reliability. References to women, whether in contemporary chronicles, in official records, or private correspondence, though relatively few and far between, do occur, and we can make at least some tentative deductions from them.

The Portuguese strongholds (*praças*) in Morocco, a chain of coastal fortified towns extending from Ceuta to Cabo de Gué at their peak in 1530, had been reduced to three by the end of the sixteenth century: Ceuta, Tangier, and Mazagão. Of these, Ceuta stayed loyal to Spain in 1640, Tangier was surrendered to the English as part of the dowry of Catherine of Braganza in 1662, and Mazagão was evacuated in 1769. The fighting in Morocco, punctuated by truces of longer or shorter duration, lasted on and off from 1415 to 1769. It partook of the character of a holy war, being regarded as a crusade on one side and a *jihad* on the other. For most of the time it was a war of petty raids and skirmishes, with cavalry detachments from the Portuguese garrisons making frequent forays into the surrounding countryside, and the Moors trying to lure them into ambushes. It was purely defensive on the Portuguese side after the last effort to take the offensive on a major scale had ended with the defeat and death of King Sebastian on the battlefield of Al Ksar al Kebir (4 August 1578).[2]

---

[1] An exception may be made for José Maria Rodrigues and Pedro de Azevedo (eds.), *Registos Paroquiais da Sé de Tanger*, I, *Casamentos de 1582 a 1678. Reconciliações de 1611 a 1622* (Lisboa, 1922), from which a trained demographer can doubtless draw some interesting conclusions.

[2] The narrative history of the Portuguese in Morocco (as distinct from the socio-economic aspects) is well covered in such works as Dom Fernando de Menezes, *Historia de Tangere* (Lisboa, 1732); J. Goulven, *La Place de Mazagan sous la domination portugaise, 1502–1769* (Paris, 1917); Joaquim Figanier, *Historia de Santa Cruz do Cabo de Gué* (Lisboa, 1945); David Lopes, *História de*

The captains of the *praças* usually had their wives and families with them, besides a number of male and female servants, slaves, and hangers-on in the form of poor relations whom they brought from Portugal. In addition there was a small resident population in each *praça*, of which Tangier was the most important. This population was basically of Portuguese origin, but there was a certain amount of inter-marriage with Moors and Berbers of both sexes who had been captured in childhood and became Christians, or who had deserted the ranks of Islam voluntarily. For most of this period, the garrisons of the *praças* only controlled the ground outside the walls which was within range of their cannon. Here they planted crops, vegetables and fruit trees, and pastured their horses and livestock. The animals were taken out every morning, when mounted scouts reported the area clear, and driven back in the evening. On occasion, raiding parties ventured some ten to twenty miles into the enemy countryside in search of booty, or of crops to burn, or of prisoners to ransom. On other occasions, the Moors raided right up to the walls, or closely besieged a *praça* for weeks or months on end.

The daily routine for the women was thus frequently broken by spells of acute anxiety, when their menfolk were out raiding, and might either return victorious with plunder, or in full flight before a superior Moorish force, or not at all. Although the Moors seldom had any siege artillery, they quite often risked frontal assaults both by day and night, and Cabo de Gué finally fell to such an onslaught after a month's siege in 1541. In these circumstances, the women often had to fight alongside their menfolk on the battlements, and the chroniclers recorded admiringly the feats of some of these impromptu Amazons. Thus when Cabo de Gué was

Arzila (Coimbra, 1924); *ibidem* in *História de Portugal. Edição Monumental*, vol. III, pp. 429–544, and vol. IV, pp. 78–129 (Barcelos, 1931–2); Cenival, Ricard, *et al.* [eds.], *Sources inédites de l'histoire du Maroc: Portugal* (5 vols, Paris, 1934–53); R. Ricard, *Études sur l'histoire des Portugais au Maroc* (Coimbra, 1955). V. Magalhães Godinho, *Historia Económica e Social da Expansão Portuguesa*, vol. I, (Lisboa, 1947) is devoted entirely to Morocco, but unfortunately was not continued in this form; the economic aspects of Portuguese expansion in Morocco are discussed exhaustively, if not always entirely convincingly, in the same author's later work, *Os descobrimentos e a economia mundial* (2 vols., Lisboa, 1963–71). Elaine Sanceau, *Castelos em Africa* (Oporto, 1961), is a good popular treatment, based mainly on Bernardo Rodrigues, *Anais de Arzila* (2 vols., ed. David Lopes, Coimbra, 1915–19), and stresses the women's part.

nearly taken by a surprise attack in 1533, 'a powerful woman, six months with child, carried on her back to rebuild the walls boulders which could not be lifted by two men, and she shouldered them as if they were nothing'. Nor did this herculean activity prevent her from giving birth to a normal child three months later.[1] On another occasion, when Arzila seemed to be on the point of falling to a fierce Moorish assault, the sagging morale of some of the garrison was revived by one of the governor's daughters, a married woman 'who was then pregnant with her belly up to her mouth with a baby girl who was born immediately afterwards'.[2] In the company of her mother and sisters, she shamed faint-hearted soldiers into returning to their posts, and seized a cross-bow with which she fired at the Moors.

Other women, of course, were not so virile nor so lucky. When Santa Cruz de Cabo de Gué was finally stormed by the Sharif of Sus in March 1541, among the prisoners was the badly-wounded captain of the fortress, Dom Goterre de Monroy and his beautiful (married) daughter Dona Mecia, who had just given birth to a girl and whose husband had just been killed. She was taken to the victor's harem, and eventually became a Muslim after giving birth to a child by him. She died soon afterwards, and the Sharif, who was genuinely devoted to her, then released her father out of compassion and waived his right to a ransom. Women on both sides were apt to be converted if they fell into the hands of the other—not so much out of harsh physical mistreatment, as of gradual pressure and persuasion. Young Moorish girls of good family who were captured by the Portuguese were usually taken into the household of the governor's wife, brought up like her own children (or servants), and, if they became Christians, married off to one of the garrison. There were, however, instances on both sides when captive women refused to be converted (or only pretended to be so), and in due course were ransomed, or made their escape. This last feat was obviously very difficult to accomplish and rarely succeeded.

In times of truce, the leaders on both sides sometimes paid each other formal visits, and on such occasions the Portuguese ladies joined in entertaining their husbands' guests, something which the

---

[1] *Apud* E. Sanceau, *Castelos em Africa*, p. 303.

[2] *prenhe e com a barriga à bôca de uma filha que logo pariu*, a strikingly evocative phrase, of which the Portuguese chroniclers were very fond (*História de Arzila*, p. 131).

Moorish ladies in their harems could never do. These instances of medieval chivalry were, however, usually confined to the 'better sort' on both sides, the common people of both sexes being given short shrift, or enslaved without further ado, instead of being allowed to live in the household of one of their equals until a ransom or exchange was arranged for them. The Portuguese commanders sometimes made no distinction between combatants and non-combatants when they got the upper hand. For instance, the captain of Safim reporting to the Crown on the result of a surprise attack made by his garrison on two Moorish encampments in July 1541 wrote: 'We took them completely by surprise and killed about 400 persons, most of them women and children. The common soldiers gave quarter to nobody, and only after they were tired of killing, did we capture some eighty souls.' The captain sought to justify this atrocity by claiming that it was a reprisal for the Moorish capture of Cabo de Gué; but although a few Portuguese women and children had been killed in the heat of battle when that stronghold was stormed, most of them had been spared.[1]

As far as women were concerned, although there were atrocities on both sides, the weight of evidence indicates that here as elsewhere the Islamic record was clearly better than the Christian. The rape of women was deeply repugnant to the strict rules of tribal warfare in most, if not all, of the Islamic world, but there were seldom any such inhibitions on the Christian side. João Carvalho Mascarenhas, a much-travelled Portuguese soldier who was captured by Algerian corsairs in 1621, and who subsequently served for several years as a galley-slave, noted that the corsairs always kept their female captives strictly segregated and allowed no sexual intercourse on board.[2] Another veteran soldier who served for many years in Portuguese Asia, also admitted that the Muslim treatment of their prisoners was often better than that of the Portuguese, and it would be very easy to adduce additional

---

[1] D. Rodrigo de Castro to King John III, Safim, 8 July 1541, in *Gulbenkiana: As Gavetas da Torre do Tombo*, I (Lisboa, 1960), p. 771. Cf. also *Studia Nr.* 33 (Lisboa, 1971), pp. 278–80; Joaquim Figanier; *História de Santa Cruz do Cabo de Gué (Agadir), 1505–1541* (Lisboa, 1945), pp. 220–3.

[2] João Carvalho Mascarenhas, *Memoravel Relaçam da perda da Nao Conceiçam que os Turcos queimarão à vista da barra de Lisboa, varios successos das pessoas, que nella cativarão de 1621 até 1626* (Lisboa, 1627), fl. 12; R. B. Serjeant, *The Portuguese off the South Arabian Coast* (Oxford, 1963), p. 31.

evidence of this.[1] Certainly, most of the women who were captured by the Moors in Morocco were eventually returned unharmed if a ransom was forthcoming, unless they had become converted to Islam as occasionally happened. Since warfare was endemic in these Moroccan *praças*, the death-rate was much higher among the male than among the female population. This also meant that widows had a good chance of remarrying, especially if they were young and not inconsolable. There was the more inducement to do this, since the chroniclers of Arzila, Tangier, and Ceuta all agree that the widowed *mulheres de Africa* ('women of Africa'), 'virtuous, chaste, and honest' as they were, often found it very difficult to receive their miserably small pensions from an admittedly impecunious Crown and from an obstructive Lisbon bureaucracy.[2]

A great contrast to the life led by the women in the embattled Moroccan *praças* was that led by those in the tropical island of São Tomé, which lies virtually on the equator in the steamy Gulf of Guinea. Uninhabited but thickly forested when first discovered by the Portuguese *circa* 1470, it was colonised during the last decade of the fifteenth century by levies of white families sent from Portugal, by some 2,000 forcibly baptised Jewish children of both sexes under nine years old, who were taken from their parents and, above all, by banished criminals and convicts (*degredados*). The island served as a slaving entrepôt for West Africans purchased on the mainland from Mina (El Mina) in present-day Ghana and in Congo and Angola. Sugar cultivation was also introduced with great success and the island had become a major producer and exporter of this crop by 1530.[3]

Those of the deported Jewish children who survived were married off as they grew up. There were about 600 of them left

---

[1] *Primor e Honra da vida soldadesca no Estado da India* (Lisboa, 1630), parte IV, fls, 107–10; C. R. Boxer, *The Portuguese Seaborne Empire, 1415–1825* (London, 1969), pp. 134–5.

[2] D. Fernando de Menezes, *Historia de Tangere* (1732), pp. 39, 81; David Lopes, *História de Arzila*, p. 259.

[3] The standard work is Francisco Tenreiro, *A ilha de São Tomé* (Lisboa, 1961), to which should be added Fernando Castelo Branco, 'O comercio de São Tomé no século XVII,' *Studia*, Nr. 24 (1968), pp. 73–98, and this author's edition of the *Actas da Camara de Santo Antonio da ilha do Príncipe, 1672–1777* (Lisboa, 1970). Robert Garfield of De Pauw University has completed a Ph.D. thesis on 'São Tomé in the 17th century', which should add greatly to our knowledge of the social history of the island.

in 1506, when an observer claimed that 'few of the women bore children of the white men; very many more bore children of the Negroes, while the Negresses bore children of the white men.' All the unmarried men were provided by the Crown with a Negress, avowedly for breeding purposes, and a marriage ceremony seems to have been optional. A Portuguese pilot who knew the island well in the second quarter of the 16th century tells us that in his day people of any European nationality were welcome to settle there. 'They all have wives and children, and some of the children who are born there are as white as ours. It sometimes happens that, when the wife of a merchant dies, he takes a Negress, and this is an accepted practice, as the Negro population is both intelligent and rich, bringing up their daughters in our way of life, both as regards custom and dress. Children born of these unions are of a dark complexion and are called Mulattoes. They are mischievous and difficult to manage.'[1]

As can be imagined, a rather peculiar society evolved in this tropical scenic paradise, but one which suffered like so much of tropical Africa from endemic malaria, here called the *carneirada*. For this and other reasons very few white women left Portugal for São Tomé between the early sixteenth century and the early twentieth century, and the mortality among white men in the island was always very high. Consequently, a mulatto élite developed within a few years and these *pardos*, as they were usually termed, were elected to serve in the municipal council or *Senado da Camara*, and nominated to ecclesiastical dignities such as canons of the local cathedral (founded in 1534), to a much greater extent than was the case elsewhere in the Portuguese empire. They also became landed proprietors or owners of *roças*, the vast sugar plantations and agricultural estates, which flourished during the sixteenth century, decayed somewhat but did not disappear in the seventeenth and eighteenth, and were changed into the thriving cocoa and coffee plantations which revived the island's economic prosperity in the nineteenth and twentieth. As has almost invariably been the case with plantations of this kind operated by slave labour, the owners of such estates tended to wax fat and kick, leading a self indulgent and despotic life which made them impatient of outside or government control—unless they themselves happened to be running the

[1] C. R. Boxer, *Race Relations in the Portuguese Empire, 1415–1825* (Oxford, 1963), p. 15.

government. Family feuds and vendettas were also common in such societies, and we get revealing glimpses of social conditions in São Tomé in a letter written by the Bishop to King John III on the 25 April 1545.[1]

The bishop relates that four days previously at about 9 or 10 a.m., a mob of infuriated women invaded the streets of the city, yelling, wailing, and shouting: 'Help here for the King! Justice! Justice!' They entered the Bishop's house in this tumultuous manner, and when the startled prelate asked them what was the matter, their spokeswoman, a *parda* 'married to a respectable white man', replied: 'Cristovão Afonso do Avelar, João Gonçalues and another man on horseback, came with many armed men to my *roça*, where I was with my husband and my widowed sister with her belly up to her mouth on the point of giving birth.[2] The aggressors took her away, dragging her off against her will, saying that they wanted to marry her with Cristovão Afonso. She shouted out "Help here for the King", and screamed that she did not want to marry him, and would never be his wife, but they carried her off by main force despite all her protests.' The Bishop told the outraged protestors that he was powerless in the matter, and that they had better go and seek redress from the local justices. The women replied that they had already tried this, but had received no satisfaction. He finally persuaded them to depart, shouting, wailing and shrieking as they had come.

The Bishop went on the explain in his letter that the justices, whether white or *pardos*, did not dare to do anything effective against the culprits, although they made a show of searching for them until news came four days later that the couple were married. Some of the authorities were friends or relatives of the aggressors, and others were afraid of them, so in the upshot nothing was or could be done. The Bishop assured the King that his scandal had created a great sensation and that nobody spoke of anything else. 'The people are so shaken by this, that they say there is now nothing else to do in São Tomé but rape women and marry them by force without fear of God or of our Lord the King.' This was certainly not the only instance when one of the local *poderosos*, backed by the

---

[1] D. Fr. João Baptista, O.P., Bishop of Utica and suffragan-bishop of São Tomé, to the King, 25 April 1545, *apud* Brásio, *Monumenta, II, 1532–1569*, pp. 128–35.

[2] *com a barriga à boca para parir*, cf. note 2, p. 14.

force of his well-armed slaves and the favour of others of his kind, successfully defied the representatives of the royal authority, sometimes for years on end.[1]

Conditions somewhat improved later, although the history of the island was an agitated one for centuries, punctuated as it was by slave revolts, three-cornered rivalry between whites, *pardos*, and free Blacks, to say nothing of French attacks and a Dutch occupation of part of the island in 1641–48. Under these circumstances, it is perhaps not surprising that the women of São Tomé no less than the men became proficient in the use of arms. Such at least is a fair deduction from the account of the island by a visiting English sea-captain, Robert Holmes, who spent four weeks there in 1664:

> 'That which I took most notice of on this unfortunate shore was that all the women were in arms, formed into companies with captains, lieutenants and ensigns in good order, and 7 or 8 companies of them. The reason is that the males do not live long upon this island, but the females do, and they have 10 females for one male.'[2]

Holmes does not state the colour of these Amazons; but given the extreme rarity of white women anywhere in West Africa at this period and for long afterwards, they must, in all probability, have been *pardas* and free Blacks. I have not come across any reference to this 'monstrous regiment of women' (*pace* John Knox) in any of the Portuguese sources; but they are very defective for this period, and Holmes can hardly have mistaken the evidence of his own eyes in such a novel matter.

Miscegenation in São Tomé had started with official encouragement, indeed compulsion would be a better term, and it continued down the centuries, taking different forms at different levels of society. So far as I know, none of the governors who were married men brought their wives from Portugal; but at least one of them who was a bachelor married in the island. This was Lourenço Pires de Tavora, acting-governor in 1628–36, who married a wealthy *parda* heiress, Ana de Chaves.[3] Other government officials likewise married into the *parda* aristocracy; but the more common

---

[1] Brásio, *Monumenta, II, 1532–1569* (1953), pp. 331–47.

[2] Richard Ollard, *Man of War. Sir Robert Holmes and the Restoration Navy* (London, 1969), p. 122.

[3] *Studia*, Nr. 30/31 (1970), pp. 260–1.

practice was for a newly arrived Portuguese to provide himself with a *lavadeira* (washerwoman) who acted as mistress and ran the household, usually providing him with children as well. The Portuguese man might, or might not, marry the *lavadeira* and legitimise his children in due course. The boys might be sent to Lisbon for their education, or even to London in the nineteenth century, and they might well settle in Europe. Those who remained in the island usually ended by marrying a darker-skinned girl, since the lighter-skinned girls preferred to take their chance of marriage, or at any rate of a steady liaison, with a white man.[2]

The *lavadeiras* who formed these more or less permanent unions should not be confused with prostitutes, although they may have originated in this way centuries ago. At any rate, a royal decree of 1559 promulgated in the name of the infant King Dom Sebastian fulminated against 'the many women who give themselves publicly for money. They live irregularly in the town alongside the married householders (*moradores casados*) and other people who lead regular lives, from which arise many scandals and bad examples and things which are a disservice to Our Lord.' Offenders were ordered to leave their present abodes and to move outside the town within fifteen days. Even there, they were not allowed to receive 'merchants and other transients who visit the island', but to confine themselves to local customers. Those who disobeyed this edict were threatened with fines and imprisonment for the first two offences, and deportation from the island to Portugal for the third offence. This might imply that they had come from Europe in the first place, but the decree is not explicit on this point.

This decree also deplored the prevailing immorality among all sections of society, including married men and the clergy, 'and thus there is great dissolution in this matter in the said city and island'. A sliding-scale of fines was imposed on offenders for the first two offences, those who maintained a mistress (*manceba*) in their house being fined more heavily than those who maintained one elsewhere. In both cases, deportation to Portugal by the first available ship would follow conviction for a third offence. Convicts who had been exiled to serve their sentence in São Tomé were excepted from this last clause, but they were thenceforth to live outside the town. Since many of these immoral women were 'leaving for the kingdom of Congo and other heathen realms',

[2] Francisco Tenreiro, *A ilha de São Tomé* (1961) pp. 199–201.

this practice was to cease forthwith; and any pilot or shipmaster found conveying such women would be fined and imprisoned as well as they. Lastly, the decree legislated against what was evidently regarded as an immodest and provocative dress, which was popular with the women of São Tomé, and was stigmatised as being 'in the heathen fashion'.[1]

As regards the implementation of these reforms, the Bishop of São Tomé wrote in reassuring terms to the Crown in April of the following year, that matters were not so bad as had been represented. The women, he said, were not so shameless that they sold themselves openly for money. He admitted that concubinage was widespread, 'but it was well-established before I came here', and he thought that things were improving, as sinners now had a greater sense of their former misdeeds. As regards the women's dress, he states that 'the principal ones and those that consider themselves respectable are all dressed after the manner and fashion of Portugal', and the use of skirts was rapidly becoming generalised. He protested that the scale of fines imposed was too high for most people to pay, so he had ventured to moderate it, 'according to the quality of the person concerned and the scandal of the offence. I am very merciful with those who confess their fault and promise amendment'. He sent most offenders to prison for a couple of days, 'because this is what they feel more than anything'. He concluded on an optimistic note by stating that 'with the grace of the Lord and with the favour of Your Highness many faults and bad customs which were in this island will be amended'.[2]

Dom Fr. Gaspar Cão, Bishop of São Tomé from 1554 to 1574, who actually resided in this fever-stricken island from 1556 to June 1565, was also no bigot, and he was given a popular ovation by crowds of well-wishers when he left the island. But the evidence on the prevailing social conditions is conflicting, to say the least, and this Bishop was formally accused of having engaged in the slave-trade, kept coloured women as his mistresses, and condoned the sexual peccadilloes of his flock, while shamelessly neglecting his pastoral duties. The Bishop stoutly denied all these allegations, which he dismissed as being the slanderous inventions of his personal enemies in the island. Far from keeping mistresses, he asserted that

[1] *Alvará* of 9 November 1559, in Brásio, *Monumenta, II, 1532–1569*, pp. 443–5.
[2] Bishop of S. Tomé to the King, 28 April 1556, in Brásio, *II*, 462–3.

he 'had never allowed a white or coloured woman to serve him in his house, and that he had taken great care to see that his doors were shut during the hours of *sesta* [midday rest] and at night.' He claimed that public and private morality had greatly improved as the result of the action which he had taken against those guilty of concubinage, and that he had not taken any bribes nor inflicted any unlawful fines. He admitted that he had received slaves from the Congo, but this was the invariable and unavoidable practice, since there was no coinage current there (other than cowries), so the bulk of his stipend was paid in this way. A judicial investigation at Lisbon cleared the Bishop on all counts, and the Crown upheld this decision by a sentence of the Cardinal-Infante Dom Henrique in 1571.[1]

What emerges from these and such other few accounts that we have of social conditions in this island, is that the *moradores* or settlers spent most of the time on their plantations (*roças*), visiting the city (in size, only a small town) occasionally. Some of these plantation-owners were wealthy women, such as the first Ana de Chaves, who founded a *morgado*, or entailed estate in 1594; but as we have no population statistics of any exactitude, I cannot say whether Captain Robert Holmes was correct in his assertion that the women of the island were much better acclimatised and so much more numerous than the men. The degree of Africanisation varied with the class involved, but there was both a *pardo* and a free Black clergy, who together were far more numerous than the white. Roman Catholicism as practised in São Tomé and the neighbouring island of Príncipe seems to have been less influenced by indigenous African beliefs than was the case, for instance, in parts of Brazil. A Carmelite friar who accompanied the Bishop of São Tomé, Dom Martinho de Ulhoa, on a pastoral visit to Príncipe in 1584, was greatly edified by the exemplary piety of the Negro slaves of both sexes and their respect for the episcopal office. 'And don't think that they do this out of simplicity,' he wrote, 'because many of them are very intelligent, and one female slave who made her confession to me actually cited a precedent from the Council of Trent.'[2] Society in São Tomé and Príncipe was clearly something *sui generis*; but it will require further research to show to what

---

[1] Sentence of the Cardinal-Infante D. Henrique, d. 14 March 1571, in Brásio, *Monumenta*, III, *1570–1599*, pp. 7–35.
[2] Letter of Fr. Diogo da Encarnação, d. 27 September 1584, *apud* Brásio, *Monumenta*, II, *1532–1569*, pp. 273–80.

extent the women in general and the *lavadeiras* in particular were responsible for the way in which it developed to the state so well described by Francisco Tenreiro.

If we have few glimpses of women, whether white, *parda*, or black, in the evolution of society in São Tomé, the position is no better for the vastly larger region of Angola during the period with which we are concerned. Previous projects for the conquest, colonisation and conversion of this region were crystallised in the charter given by the Crown in 1571 to Paulo Dias de Novais, a grandson of the discoverer of the Cape of Good Hope. This charter was drawn up on the lines of those previously awarded to the *donatários* or lords-proprietors for the settlement of coastal Brazil. Dias was appointed hereditary proprietor of a projected colony extending from the mouth of the River Kwanza to about 170 miles southwards along the coast and to an indefinite extent landwards. Among his responsibilities was the settlement of one hundred Portuguese peasant families, provided with 'all the seeds and plants which they can take with them from this kingdom and from the island of São Tomé', within the space of six years. But when Paulo Dias' expedition arrived with the pioneer colonists off Luanda in 1575, the slave-trade with São Tomé had already been flourishing for over fifty years. Malaria and other tropical diseases proved an insuperable obstacle to white colonisation then and for the next three centuries. The high ideals of the royal charter were forthwith abandoned for the unrestrained procurement of *peças* (*lit.* 'pieces'), as Negro slaves were termed.

White women were at a premium in Angola and its capital of São Paulo de Luanda for over three centuries. The place had the reputation of being a 'white man's grave', as did virtually all of West Africa, and very few Portuguese men who went there took their wives along. The first governor to do so was Dom Antonio de Lencastre, who brought his wife and daughters with him from Portugal in 1772. In 1593, the Crown for the first time sent out to Luanda a group of twelve *orfãas del Rei*, the 'orphans of the King', white girls of marriageable age from orphanages at Lisbon and Oporto. Each girl was provided with a dowry in the form of some minor government post for whoever decided to marry her. This system was even less of a success in Angola than it was in Portuguese India, where it was tried out over a much longer period and more methodically as we shall see (pp. 66–7 *infra*). We have scattered references to other such annual shipments, which indicate that the practice continued for some decades, although with considerable irregularity. In 1664, however, the *Senado da Camara* or Municipal Council of Luanda asked the Crown not to send any more white girls or women, whether bona fide orphans or reclaimed prostitutes, to be married in Angola. They pointed out that there were plenty of marriageable females in the colony owing to their fathers and/or husbands having been killed during the Dutch war and occupation of Luanda and Benguela in 1641-8.[1]

Our best single source for the style of life in Angola and Luanda during the seventeenth century is the soldier-chronicler, António de Oliveira Cadornega, who spent over forty years in the colony (1639-85), and who served in the municipal councils of Massangano and Luanda. He tells us in his classic *General History of the Angolan Wars* (*História Geral das Guerras Angolanas*), which he compiled at Luanda in 1680-83, that with the exception of a few married couples who had come out with the first *conquistadores* in the 1570s, most of the subsequent arrivals were men who 'accommodated themselves with Mulatas, daughters of worthy men and conquerors who had begotten them either on their female slaves or on free Negro women. Many of their descendants are both honourable and noble, and can be compared in this way with those of India and the State of Brazil: those of India descending from the time when the great Afonso de Albuquerque made those [inter-racial] marriages in the city of Goa, capital of that Indian Empire, for the further increase of that populous city and State, marrying many of the principal men who accompanied him with the female peoples of that East, from whom we see descended today a very aristocratic (*fidalga*) generation. The same thing happened subsequently in Brazil with its *camarus* and *mamelucos*, and in Angola with its mulattoes and *pardos*, for these have come to be the native-born of these lands.'[2]

Cadornega admitted, however, that the chief demographic

---

[1] Ralph Delgado, *História de Angola* (4 vols., Benguela and Lobito, 1948-1955), vol. I, p. 360; C. R. Boxer, *Portuguese Society in the Tropics. The Municipal Councils of Goa, Macao, Bahia and Luanda, 1510-1800* (University of Wisconsin Press, 1965), pp. 128-9, and the sources there quoted.

[2] José Matias Delgado and Manuel da Cunha (eds.), *História Geral das Guerras Angolanas* (3 vols, Lisboa, 1950-2), vol. III, pp. 28-30. *Camarus* and *mamelucos* refer to various forms of Brazilian mixed-bloods, the latter being usually defined as the offspring of a white man and an Amerindian mother.

contribution to Luanda came not so much from the respectable married citizens with their families of mixed blood, but from the soldiers, sailors, merchants and other transients mating 'with black ladies for lack of white ladies'. These unions, which were obviously fleeting and irregular, gave rise to a large mulatto and coloured population, many of which formed a lumpen-proletariat. Others, however, made good soldiers, since they were much more resistant to tropical diseases than the (mostly unwilling) conscripts from Portugal, Madeira, and the Azores. They could also endure the hardships of warfare in the *sertão* or backlands more easily.

Reverting to the better class of citizens, Cadornega noted that the women and girls 'live longer in this kingdom, since they are not exposed to the calamities of the sun and the hardships of the backlands', as their menfolk were when they had to participate in the frequent campaigns against unsubdued or rebellious African tribes. One may suspect that another reason was that they led less irregular lives than their husbands, brothers and fathers, who had uninhibited sexual freedom; whereas they had none, at any rate in theory. Cadornega himself must have been something of an exception and a record, living as he did for over forty years in this notoriously unhealthy place. But even his clearly exceptional stamina was far surpassed by that of a white woman, Violante Alvarez, who came from Vila Viçosa, the same town in Portugal as he did. She lived to attain the age of 120 years in Luanda (so he claims), 'and she had so many descendants that she used to say "Granddaughter, bring your grand-daughter here!" And despite her great age, she had all her teeth in her mouth and she could crack an olive-stone with them.'[1]

Cadornega also tells us of another remarkable Portuguese matron, Isabel da Rocha, who was married no fewer then seven times in the frontier fortress of Cambambe. When the body of her sixth husband was lying in state in the house before being taken off to the cemetery, she was approached on behalf of a prospective suitor, but replied that it was too late, as she had already become engaged to another—her seventh and last husband who survived her.[2] Cadornega mentions admiringly 'a valorous matron, Joana Gomes, who was gigantic in both body and bravery', whose

[1] Cadornega, *História das Guerras Angolanas*, vol. III, p. 314.
[2] Cadornega, *História das Guerras Angolanas*, vol. II, p. 153 and vol. III, pp. 314–15.

feats in the defense of the fortress of Muxima against the Dutch in 1646 he compared with those of the heroines in the first great siege of Diu over a century previously.[1] These remarkable women would clearly have been exceptions in any society; but their existence goes to show that although white women were very few on the ground in Angola, they might be in a position to exert a very considerable influence on their husbands, their children, and their slaves.

Equally exceptional was the career of another white woman whom Cadornega knew in Angola. The Dutch wife of a Dutch soldier during their occupation of Luanda, she had been sent to the *quilombo* or war-camp of the famous cannibal Queen Jinga (Nzinga Amona), who had asked the Dutch governor of Luanda to send her a white woman, presumably for exhibition as part of her entourage. When this *quilombo* was stormed by a Portuguese flying-column in March 1646, Queen Jinga, the Dutch woman's husband and their little boy escaped. The wretched woman, in the last stages of pregnancy and sobbing bitterly, was found by the victorious Portuguese, of whom Cadornega was one. He relates that she forthwith gave birth to a baby boy who was promptly baptised as a Roman Catholic. The mother followed suit, 'and is still alive in our fortress and garrison-town of Cambambe', but whether she remarried he does not say.[2]

A third category of women who came to Angola, especially during the eighteenth century, was composed (like the *degredados*) of those who were convicted criminals, in the same way as the English shipped thousands of female convicts to Australia in the late eighteenth and early nineteenth centuries. The Portuguese, or the Luso-Brazilian women who were sent to serve their sentences in Angola, were nothing like so numerous, but there was apparently a constant trickle of them. As usual, complete statistics are wanting, but from partially complete records which have survived for the years 1714–48, we can see that they included married women,

---

[1] Cadornega, *História das Guerras Angolanas*, vol. I, pp. 477–8. For the heroines of Diu see Teresa Leitão de Barros, *As heroínas de Diu* (Lisboa, 1954).

[2] Cadornega, *História das Guerras Angolanas*, vol. I, p. 413. For the background to this campaign see David Birmingham, *Trade and Conflict in Angola: the Mbundu and their neighbours under the influence of the Portuguese, 1483–1790* (Oxford, 1966), pp. 104–9; Jan Vansina, *Kingdoms of the Savanna* (University of Wisconsin Press, 1966), pp. 134–7, 142–3.

widows, spinsters, slaves, and even unfortunate little gypsy children who were shipped off together with their parents. As with the more numerous male convicts, murderers seem to have got off comparatively lightly, whereas thieves, gypsies and vagrants often received life-sentences. Thus, Maria Gomes Pimental, 'a tall coloured woman' from Villa Nova da Rainha in Brazil, was sentenced to only ten years' banishment in Angola for being a willing accomplice in the murder of her husband; whereas two little gypsy girls, aged respectively five and ten, were sentenced to banishment for life together with their widowed mother, merely for being gypsies.[1]

One of the marked differences between the Spanish (rather, the Castilian) Crown and the Portuguese Crown was that the former rarely shipped levies of convicted criminals to serve their sentences overseas, whereas the latter made a regular annual practice of it. Another great difference was the comprehensive legislation enacted by the Castilian Crown to compel erring or absconding husbands to return to their wives in Spain, or to send for them to join them in America; whereas the Portuguese Crown seldom legislated at all on this matter and then only in individual cases. On the contrary, it often actively discouraged women from emigrating with (or going to join) their husbands in Asia or in Africa, although it was more complacent about Brazil. Further discussion of this attitude will be in place later (pp. 64–7 *infra*), but I will cite here one instance from Angola.

In 1625, the Governor of Angola, Fernão de Sousa, complained to the Crown that the Bishop wanted to deport to Portugal all the married men who had not got their wives with them in the African colony, 'in order to make them live with their wives'. The governor alleged that this was an infringement of the liberty of the subject, and he strongly objected to the Bishop's proposal. As the King at this time was a Castilian (Philip IV of Spain, III of Portugal), the Board of Conscience and Orders to whom the problem was referred for their advice came up with a compromise decision. Married men who had been in Angola for a longer time than they were supposed to be, and who were not government officials, should be deported by the Governor and Bishop if they would not return

---

[1] In C. R. Boxer, *Portuguese Society in the Tropics*, (1965), p. 202. The severity with which crimes against property were punished was common to most European jurisprudence at this time.

voluntarily.[1] One may doubt if this ruling, which was accepted by the Crown, had the slightest effect. I can recall no instance of a married Portuguese being deported from Angola (or from any other part of Africa) 'to live a married life with his wife'—*fazer vida marital com a sua mulher*, as the stock expression was.

With such a disparity between the numbers of white men and women, it is not surprising that the Africanisation of European society in Luanda, which was beginning to be noticeable in Cadornega's day and generation, had progressed much further a century later. A Brazilian officer who served in the garrison during the 1780s describes the ladies of Luanda as speaking Ambundo with their slaves and with each other in preference to Portuguese. 'They are verbose in family conversations but are mute in polite assemblies.' As for their husbands: 'The men speak Portuguese and are fluent in Ambundo.' The wife of the Baron of Mossamedes, who was the Governor-General of Angola from 1784 to 1790, tried to improve the standard of female elegance and culture by persuading the women to dress in the European style. To this end, she took some girls from the principal families into Government House, 'whom she educated in European precepts and manners, teaching them sewing, embroidery, reading, writing, arithmetic, music, dancing, and, as a result, to speak'. She organised elegant assemblies and gave polite parties; but Captain Elias Alexandre da Silva Corrêa feared that after her departure they would abandon such civilised accomplishments, 'although they are intelligent enough to be able to cultivate them to perfection'.[2] He was not far wrong; but it was not until the next century that the trend towards complete Africanisation was first stopped and then reversed.

Having glanced at women in two societies which experienced a greater or lesser degree of Africanisation over the centuries, let us take a brief look at an island society where nothing of the kind was involved, although slavery existed there. As mentioned previously, the Azores were discovered, or rediscovered, *c.* 1431–52—it does not matter which, since they were uninhabited when first settled and

---

[1] *Consulta da Mesa da Consciencia*, 2 October 1625, with Crown's decision of 3 June 1626, in Brásio, *Monumenta*, *VII, 1622–1630*, pp. 386–8.

[2] Elias Alexandre da Silva Corrêa, *Historia de Angola, 1782–95* (2 vols, Lisboa, 1937), vol. I, pp. 82–3; vol. II, p. 152. For the sorry state of Luanda and Angola at this period, cf. J. Gentil da Silva, 'En Afrique Portugaise: L'Angola au XVIIIᵉ siècle', *Annales*, vol. XIV (Paris, 1959), pp. 571–80.

colonised. Despite the great fertility of their volcanic soil, in places where the terrain permits of cultivation, and the healthiness of their temperate if humid climate, the colonisation of these islands proceeded rather slowly at first, even though they attracted families from Flanders as well as from Portugal. The rhythm varied in the different islands, but the real impulse and increment of the population in São Muguel, the largest and most fertile, dates from the period 1474–1522. By 1525, this island had six towns, and 4,000 or 5,000 persons are said to have perished in the earthquake which devastated the (then) capital, Villa Franca, in that year. Existence was easy, but conditions of life remained simple for the first half of the sixteenth century. The land produced wheat, wine, and livestock in abundance. But there were no schools, insufficient clergy, and relatively little seaborne trade with Portugal or elsewhere. Rustic simplicity and modest comfort were enjoyed by most people. Since nearly everyone was engaged in agriculture, there was no great social distinction between the various classes until the second half of the sixteenth century, when there was a great expansion in the foreign trade of the island, with wheat exports to Lisbon, and woad (*pastel*) for blue dye to England, France and Flanders. It was then that the formation of the *morgados* (entailed estates) began, and these have been a feature of the island ever since.[1]

Mutatis mutandis, the other islands with their staple products (wine in Pico, wheat in Terceira, for example), also flourished at the same period; particularly Terceira, which, with its port of Angra, was at the cross-road of the shipping routes from America and from the East, thus affording scope for contraband as well as for legitimate trade. Jesuit colleges were established at Angra (1570), Ponta Delgada (1636), and Faial (1652), reflecting the rise in prosperity and the standard of living. At the end of the sixteenth century, São Miguel had five towns besides the city of Ponta Delgada, and 97 churches with some 104 secular clergy, apart from those of the Religious Orders, to serve a total population of 40,000, distributed among 5,667 households. There was a militia of 5,000 infantry and

[1] Gaspar Frutuoso, *Saudades da Terra* (ed. João Bernardo Oliveira Rodrigues, Ponta Delgada, 1963–68). For the position of the Azores in the geography and economy of the Atlantic world cf. Frédéric Mauro, *Le Portugal et l'Atlantique au XVIIᵉ siècle, 1570–1670* (Paris, 1960); T. Bentley Duncan, *Madeira, The Azores and the Cape Verdes in 17th century commerce and navigation* (Chicago University Press, 1972).

600 cavalry, apart from the garrison of Ponta Delgada. The taxes on this island brought the Crown an annual income of over 50,000 *cruzados*, which was more than that of all the other eight islands of the Azores put together. I have no figures for the slave population; but it was probably less than that of Madeira, with its sugar industry and its closer proximity to Africa, where the island capital of Funchal contained some 3,000 Negro and Mulatto slaves of both sexes in 1552, 'pelo rol da confissão'.

The life of the Portuguese women in these islands naturally closely resembled that of their sisters in Portugal itself. This by all accounts was not usually very lively, at any rate among the upper classes. Even the Spaniards made fun of the jealous and harem-like seclusion in which most Portuguese fathers of families kept their wives and daughters; and visitors from Northern Europe never failed to comment on this side of Portuguese social life. There were exceptions, of course; but most Portuguese husbands would probably have agreed with the Bishop who said that the highest intellectual task of which a woman was capable was to arrange a chest of linen properly.[1] This point will be elaborated in the final lecture, but it will suffice to note here that some of this upper-class attitude was naturally followed by the working-class, although the rigorous seclusion of the wives and daughters of farmers, peasants and fishermen was quite impracticable. A visiting English seaman at Lisbon in 1661 gives an interesting characterisation of 'the inhabitants and their ways', which it is worth quoting in full here, as indicative of the background from which came so many of those overseas:

> 'The inhabitants are Papists, not loving a Protestant very well, but indifferent good of nature, and are black [i.e. dark] of complexion, and their womenkind are very fair and handsome and having very pretty children. And also there are in this city many courtesans, many of them both young and handsome, who will call any Englishman or strangers as they walk the streets, and will ask them in as good English as they can speak whether they

---

[1] '. . . A mulher que mais sabe, não passa de saber arrumar hũa arca de roupa branca', *apud* Dom Francisco Manuel de Mello, *Carta de Guia de Casados*, Lisboa 1651, p. 79 *verso*) 'Do homem a praça, da mulher a casa', 'O marido barca, a mulher arca', 'Homem barca mulher arca' were others of Dom Francisco's favourite aphorisms.

will come in and drink the wine and take a bit to stay their longing; sitting and looking out of their windows upon who passeth by, and they are decked very handsome in apparel and gorny [?] in their hair, finely dressed with ribbons and open sleeves and buttoned jackets, their shifts being as large as half-shirts in England, very neat and handsome.

'But the men that are married are given much to jealousy, and will not permit any stranger to come where their wives are, much less to see them, but will keep them out of sight as much as possibly they can, not suffering them to go to fairs and markets as they do in England; but will go themselves and buy what is to be bought, such as provisions and other necessaries. But they allow brothel-houses, and will give their sons money or leave to go to them sooner than to the tavern, for they say "Let them be drunk and they are apt to all manner of vice", for you shall seldom see any of them drunk. But their daughters they keep always at home under their mother's custody, not suffering them to go when and where they please at the beck of their sweethearts, which is too common a use with us in England, and to the undoing of many a good man's son or daughter. They seldom go anywhere but to the church or sometimes take the fresh air with their parents or other overseers: and all their women, both married and unmarried, go with a black veil over their heads and reaching down to their legs, all being covered except their eyes.' On another voyage four years later, Barlow's ship called at São Miguel, where he noted 'that the Portugal women are counted the finest needle-women in the world, doing more for twopence than an Englishwoman will do for a shilling'.[1]

Other facets of the lives and attitudes of women in the Azores can be deduced from a study of their last wills and testaments in the local archives. I have only been able to work there for two short periods, but these records afford some interesting comparisons with those relating (for example) to Bahia, Goa, and Macao. Thus on her deathbed at Faial on 19 July 1534, the Lady Isabel Corte-Real, described as *Capitoa* of the island, freed all her slaves, male and female, 'save only two, called Diogo and Miranda. All the others

[1] Basil Lubbock (ed.), *Barlow's Journal of his life at Sea in King's Ships, East and West Indiamen and other merchantmen from 1659 to 1703* (2 vols., London, 1934), vol. I, pp. 63, 88.

belonging to me, I leave free, and without any burden of slavery, to go freely today in peace wherever it seems best to each and every one of them.' She was the wife of Jos Dutra Corte-Real, Captain and Governor of Faial and Pico; but she was illiterate and had to get someone to sign for her.

The *capitoa*, although she freed all but two of her slaves on her deathbed, did not, it seems, make any provision for them, but left them to make their own way in the world. Other owners were more considerate. They sometimes left their manumitted bondservants small sums of money, or pieces of household furniture, or clothing, to help them start life afresh. Lucas Cacena (or Cassena), a wealthy *fidalgo* and merchant of Italian origin, who made his will at Angra on the 12 September 1538, freed, among others, two Mulatto slaves, and bequeathed a sum of 10,000 *reis* in ready money to each of them, 'para supprimento de sua vida'. The same testator freed a female slave named Galharda, leaving her likewise 10,000 *reis* 'to buy a slave, and 5,000 *reis* to buy a dress'. A more common practice, which Lucas Cacena also did with several of his other slaves, was to free them conditionally, provided that they continued in the service of another member of the family for a term of years, varying in this instance from two to twenty.[1]

Lucas Cacena was an exceptionally large slave-owner for the time and place—he mentions at least ten by name in his will—but most of the other testators whose wills I have examined owned only one or two, if they had any at all. Even so, they usually made some mention of their slaves, either freeing them entirely, or, more often, conditionally. Manuel Peres, who made his will at Angra on 8 June 1616, bequeathed his Negress slave, Helena, to his sister; but he stipulated that Helena should be allowed to keep her bed and her clothes 'which she regarded as her own', as she had been allowed to do by the testator's mother with his permission. Servants as well as slaves were naturally remembered in wills.[2] Vasco Fernandes Redovalho, who made his will at Angra on 29 July 1544, besides freeing his slave 'Pedro Fernandez, a Black from Guinea who has served me faithfully, on condition that he serves my lady wife for the rest of her life', also bequeathed the sum of 5,000 *reis*

[1] 'Livro do Tombo do Convento de São Francisco de Angra' (MSS. dated 1633 in the Public Library and Archive of Angra, Terceira, Azores), fls. 62–3, 56–58.

[2] 'Livro do Tombo do Convento de São Francisco de Angra', fls. 23–5.

to Brigida, a 'maid who was brought up in my household, in order to help her get married'.[1]

Several testators, inflicted with belated pangs of conscience on their death-beds, tried to discharge outstanding debts, however old or however small. Vidal de Bettencourt de Vasconcellos, a leading *fidalgo* of Angra, who drew up his will on the 24 April 1628, stated: 'I declare that I had in my household during the time of my late wife, Dona Ignes, a girl called Maria Soares, who died in the year of the Plague [1599] in the local Hospital, to whom I owed 20,000 *reis*, and I want my executors to try to trace any heirs that this girl may have and to pay them this sum, and also some more money which I owed her for the years she served me, but I cannot recall how much . . .' This gentleman was evidently neglectful about paying his servants, for he went on to enumerate another girl, 'called the Albernaz, whom I have not paid because she is still a minor'; so he left instructions for her to be paid in full as well as a third maid to whom wages were owing. He also liquidated an old if minute debt by ordering his executors to pay a debt of five *tostões* (about 30 shillings English) 'to the widow of Alvaro Gonçalves, Cooper, who lives in Pernambuco'.[2]

Of course, the bulk of these wills and testaments are not concerned so much with slaves and servants as with members of the testators' family, whether spouse or children, and with bequests to churches, convents, or charitable foundations, which were more or less obligatory in the deeply religious society of the time. They do not differ in essence from those which have been analysed elsewhere, such as in John Russell-Wood's admirable *Fidalgos and Philanthropists: The Santa Casa da Misericórdia of Bahia, 1550–1755* (1968).[3] Prior emphasis was usually placed on the number of masses to be said for the testator's soul; and where possible, provision was made for an unmarried daughter, unless the girl was already in a convent. Admission to a convent usually required a *dote* (dowry), sometimes a very substantial one, and parents often made considerable sacrifices in this way. It would also be interesting to study these records to ascertain the percentage of literacy among the women concerned at different periods. One would expect this to be pretty low; but I have the impression that a fair number were literate and (as one might

---

[1] 'Livro do Tombo do Convento de São Francisco de Angra', fls. 69–70.
[2] 'Livro do Tombo do Convento de São Francisco de Angra', fls. 386.
[3] Cf. especially pp. 146–200.

3

expect) most of the nuns were, presumably because they came from better class families as a general rule. Another aspect which I feel would repay further research would be the role of women, whether widows or heiresses, in the formation and management of the *morgados* or entailed estates, particularly those of the island of São Miguel, where the documentation seems to be abundant and the researchers at present few.[2]

[2] The staff is both competent and helpful, as I can vouch from personal experience at Ponta Delgada (1970) and Angra (1972).

CHAPTER TWO

Spanish and Portuguese America

Columbus took no women with him on his famous voyage of discovery in 1492. This is hardly surprising; but it is rather odd that there were none accompanying the 1,500 men who sailed on the second expedition. They left Cadiz on 23 September 1493, in seventeen ships laden with supplies of livestock, seeds, and plants, for starting a European colony in the New World. Provision was made for thirty women to be embarked in the ships of Columbus's third voyage (1497–8), and these, or those of them who actually sailed, were presumably the first Spanish women to cross the Atlantic. From then onwards, a steady trickle of females came every year, but it never amounted to a flood, and all estimates of the volume are largely guesswork. Tabulations for the Indies as a whole, based mainly on the incomplete lists of *Pasajeros a Indias*, have indicated a ratio of about ten men for every woman. Richard Konetzke and other scholars have pointed out that the actual proportion of women in Spanish America must have been higher than it had been at any given time of emigration, because of the greater mortality among the men.[1] Their distribution also varied widely in place and time, for obvious reasons. But after the conquest period was over, they were probably most numerous in Mexico, less so in Peru, and virtually absent in remote frontier regions such as Paraguay. In any event, as Lockhart has pointed out, large regions of Spanish America had enough European women to enable them to retain their Iberian culture and traditions intact[2]: as opposed to many Portuguese settlements that had very few or none, and where the Portuguese language, religion, and culture were drastically diluted, as we have seen and will see in the course of these lectures.

It need hardly be said that the sailors left behind by Columbus at La Navidad on his first voyage (all of whom were killed by the long-suffering Arawaks before his return, mainly due to their seizing native women), nor the fifteen hundred males on the second voyage,

[1] James Lockhart, *Spanish Peru, 1532–1560: A Colonial Society* (University of Wisconsin Press, 1968), pp. 150–2, 261 and the sources there quoted.
[2] James Lockhart, *Spanish Peru*, p. 226.

waited in sexual continence for women to come from Spain to join them. They 'shacked up'—often literally—with the Arawak women of their choice (to use another Americanism), and with or without the permission, connivance, or refusal of their menfolk. At this period, race-prejudice in the Iberian Peninsula was concentrated against the 'Moors' (e.g. Muslims) and the Jews, mainly for religious reasons; although Africans tended to be despised because of their connection with slavery, being 'bought and sold like cattle', as King Afonso V of Portugal told a visiting Bohemian knight in 1467.[1] A royal instruction of March 1503, sent to Nicolas de Ovando, who had replaced Columbus as Governor of the Indies, urged the colonial authorities not only to persuade the Arawak men to marry with their wives 'in the face of Holy Mother Church', but also to try to arrange inter-racial marriages (as opposed to concubinage) between Europeans and Amerindians of both sexes. This was reinforced by another royal order of October 1514, which reiterated that European Spaniards could freely marry with 'the native women of the said island [Hispaniola] without incurring any fault thereby'.[2]

Nor were these exhortations encouraging inter-racial marriage without effect. Carl Ortwin Sauer has used contemporary reports to show that in 1514, wives from Castile [better, Spain] were present in all save one of the fourteen towns which had been established in Hispaniola, and that about one married Spaniard in three had an Amerindian wife. As he says: 'Families of white and legitimate mestizo offspring were being started and thereby the first roots were put down into the soil of the New World. These were the founding fathers and mothers of a permanent colony.'[3]

Of course this development varied from island to island in the Antilles, or in such of them as were colonised, for the Spaniards made no efforts to occupy them all. With the conquest of Mexico and Peru, many Spanish and Creole families emigrated to the

[1] Malcolm Letts (ed.), *The Travels of Leo of Rozmital, 1465–1467* (Cambridge, 1957), p. 106.

[2] '. . . e que ansi mismo procure que algunos cristianos se casen con algunas mujeres Indias, e las mujeres cristianas con algunos Indios' (*cédula real* of 29 March 1503, *apud* José María Ots Capdequí, *Instituciones Sociales de la America Española en el periodo colonial* (La Plata, 1934), p. 119).

[3] Carl Ortwin Sauer, *The Early Spanish Main* (University of California Press, 1966), pp. 199–200, for detailed breakdown by townships of the 93 Castilian (Spanish) wives and the 54 Amerindian.

mainland and they were not replaced by adequate numbers of new arrivals from Spain. In Hispaniola itself, and later in Cuba, Puerto Rico and Jamaica, the aboriginal inhabitants were extirpated and their place taken by West African Negro slaves. Many of these latter gained their freedom in the course of time, and there was much concubinage and some inter-marriage between Europeans, Africans and *mestizos* (or *mestizas*). This race mixture had already gone too far to be stopped when the Crown endeavoured to legislate against it, with the increasing craze for *limpieza de sangre* (purity of blood) in Old Spain itself and its reflection in the Indies.

In 1687, the Castilian Crown received a complaint from the city-fathers of Santo Domingo (Hispaniola) that many members of the garrison 'with a certain rank' (*determinada categoria*, probably junior officers or non-commissioned officers) were marrying with 'Black women and Mulatas'. This development was regarded askance by the local gentry, because women who had formerly been their family slaves, by contracting these marriages now became the lawful wives of 'their hierarchical superiors in the military sphere'. The Crown gave a somewhat ambiguous reply, to the effect that the military men who made these undesirable marriages would not, in future, be promoted above a certain rank (*determinada categoria*), but it did not specify what that rank actually should be. The Crown also gave the offenders an escape-hatch, by stating that if they were individuals with long and faithful service, they could appeal through the Governor of the island to have their case for promotion laid before the *Junta de Guerra de Indias* at Madrid. A similar complaint about the tendency of many military men to marry undesirable local women without obtaining leave from the Crown was made by the Governor of Puerto Rico over half a century later, in 1746. He gave as the reason for this regrettable state of affairs that the men in question were badly paid, adding that they usually 'married with mulatas or women of the lowest social class' (*mujeres mulatas o de ínfima condición social*), which implies that the offenders were soldiers and non-commissioned officers rather than officers.[1]

---

[1] *Cédulas reales* of 2 Sept. 1687 and 4 July 1746, in José Maria Ots, *Instituciones Sociales* (1934), pp. 140–1. Cf. also the curious *dictamen* of Dr Fembra, delivered in Mexico 1752, on unequal marriages involving a person's class, or race, or both, in Verena Martinez-Alier, 'Elopement and Seduction in 19th-century Cuba' (*Past and Present*, Nr. 55, May, 1972, pp. 91–129, especially p. 91).

Inter-racial marriages always continued, whether actually encouraged, tolerated, deprecated, or strictly forbidden, as varied with
time, place, and the social category of the individuals concerned.
However, there is no doubt but that from the days of the Conquest,
most successful Spaniards in the New World aspired to have a
white wife as the legitimate female head of their household. A few
inter-marriages which took place between Aztec or Inca princesses
and leading (but never *the* leading) *conquistadores* do not invalidate
this generalisation. The men might not always want the particular
'girls they left behind them' in Old Spain, but a Spanish wife was a
major status symbol, apart from anything else. From the early
sixteenth century, the Castilian Crown legislated emphatically and
often that married men in America must either send for their wives,
once they had settled down, or else return to Spain 'to live a married
life' with them there. The frequent repetition of such orders is proof
that they were far from being universally obeyed, as Veitia Linaje
complained in 1672. But the fact remains that many married men
did fetch or send for their absent wives, however belatedly—sometimes after fifteen or twenty years.[1]

The Castilian Crown also legislated against unmarried girls going
out to the Indies, unless as members of the family of an emigrant or
an official posted to the colonies, or a maid-servant employed by
such. This rule was often and easily evaded, as it was not difficult for
an enterprising girl in search of a husband overseas to pass herself
off as a relation or a servant of some authorised and complacent
male head of a household. In any event, the head of the family
and his wife were entitled to bring not only their own daughters
but nieces and cousins as well. When the *Adelantado*, Don Pedro de
Alvarado, returned to Guatemala in 1538 with his new bride,
they brought a large company of retainers and dependents, including many ladies and serving women, as well as an elderly widower
with nine children to find places for in the New World. It was on
this occasion that the celebrated argument occurred among the
marriageable young ladies as to whether it would be advisable to
marry a battle-scarred old *conquistador* in the knowledge that he
would soon die, and leave the rich young widow free to get a young

---

[1] A number of the relevant *cédulas* are cited by José María Ots, *Instituciones
Sociales* (1934), pp. 183–90; and compare Don Joseph de Veitia Linage, *Norte
de la Contratacion de las Indias Occidentales* (Seville, 1672), libro I, cap. 29;
libro II, cap. 1.

man of her own age—an attitude which so disgusted a veteran *conquistador* who overheard the discussion, that he promptly returned home 'and called a priest, and was married to a noble Indian woman, by whom he already had two natural children'.[1]

Since most Viceroys and high officials brought their families with them when they came, and there were many well-educated Spanish and Creole ladies in the principal cities of Spanish America, such as Mexico City, Guatemala, Lima and Potosí, an elegant and civilised society developed in which women could and did play a more prominent part than they could in the Portuguese colonial settlements. There were brilliant vice-regal courts at Mexico City and Lima, far exceeding anything that could be found in Portuguese or in English America during the seventeenth century. Perhaps the most famous Mexican woman of the colonial period was Soror Juana Inés de la Cruz, who has been called 'the most important literary figure of colonial Hispanic America'. A precocious child, with an insatiable curiosity, she first entered a convent in 1667, and two years later took the veil at the age of eighteen. Intellectually she was superior to the society in which she moved, whether inside or outside her lavishly furnished cell, with its library of over 4,000 volumes. Apart from her numerous poetical works, she had a good knowledge of languages, philosophy, theology, astronomy and painting, and was termed 'the Tenth Muse'. At the age of fourteen she more than held her own in a confrontation with forty of the most learned men of Mexico City. She was a feminist before her time, and though greatly admired and respected by all who knew her, she resented her inability to make men feel more appreciative of the intellectual potential of women in general, 'those poor souls who are generally considered so inept'.[2] In an ode of 1683 addressed to another blue-stocking, the Portuguese-born Duchess of Aveiro at Madrid, Soror Juana extolled the latter for proving that intelligence had nothing to do with sex (... *que probáis que no es el sexo de la inteligencia parte*).

Less remembered nowadays, but almost equally famous in her

[1] Related on the authority of the Inca Garcilasso in W. L. Schurz, *This New World* (ed. 1956), pp. 291–2.

[2] W. L. Schurz, *This New World* (ed. 1956), pp. 320–1, 337, and the sources there quoted, to which should be added her collected works edited by Alfonso Méndez Plancarte (4 vols. Mexico, 1951–7), and R. Ricard, 'Antonio Vieira et Sor Juana Inés de la Cruz', in *Bulletin des Études Portugaises* (Coimbra, 1948).

own day and generation, was Doña Juana Maldonado de Paz, daughter of an *Oidor* (High Court Judge) at Guatemala, who was also called 'the Tenth Muse'. The renegade English Dominican friar, Thomas Gage, gives us an interesting glimpse of her in *The English American. A new survey of the West Indies* (1648):

'This Dona Juana de Maldonado y Paz was the wonder of all that cloister, yea of all the city for her excellent voice, and skill in music, and in carriage, and education yielded to none abroad nor within. She was witty, well spoken, and above all a Calliope, or Muse for ingenious and sudden verses; which the Bishop[1] said so much moved him to delight in her company and conversation. Her father[2] thought nothing too good, nor too much for her; and therefore having no other children, he daily conferred upon her riches, as might best beseem a nun, as rich and costly cabinets faced with gold and silver, pictures and idols [*sic*] for her chamber with crowns and jewels to adorn them; which with other presents from the Bishop (who dying in my time left not wherewith to pay his debts, for that as the report went, he had spent himself and given all unto this nun) made this Dona Juana de Maldonado so rich and stately, that at her own charges she built for herself a new quarter within the cloister with rooms and galleries, and a private garden-walk, and kept at work and to wait on her half a dozen blackamoor maids; but above all she placed her delight in a private chapel or closet to pray in, being hung with rich hangings, and round about it costly *laminas* (as they call them) or pictures painted upon brass set in black ebony frames with corners of gold, some of silver, brought to her from Rome. Her altar was accordingly decked with jewels, candlesticks, crowns, lamps, and covered with a canopy embroidered with gold. In her closet she had a small organ, and many sorts of musical instruments, whereupon she played sometimes by herself, sometimes with her best friends of the nuns; and here especially she entertained with music her beloved the Bishop. Her chapel or place of devotion was credibly reported about the city to be worth at least 6,000 crowns, which was enough for a

[1] Don Fr. Juan Zapata y Sandoval, O.S.A., Bishop of Guatemala, December 1621 to January 1630, when he died.
[2] Juan Maldonado de Paz, successively *Fiscal* (1609-13) and *Oidor* (1613-31) of Guatemala, then transferred to Mexico, where he died.

nun that had vowed chastity, poverty, and obedience. But all this after her decease she was to leave to the cloister.'[1]

By way of contrast to these two charming and intellectual nuns of the seventeenth century, we may consider an illiterate slave girl, who never managed to speak Spanish properly in the course of her long life, but who died in the odour of sanctity, at least in the opinion of her numerous devotees in all classes of society. Catarina de San Juan, popularly known as *La China Poblana*, was an outstanding examplar of that excessively devout type of woman known in Iberian society as the *beata*. Born at some unascertained date around 1600–10, in what is now Bangladesh, she was kidnapped as a child by the half-caste Portuguese pirates who harassed the Ganges Delta, taken to Cochin, where she was baptized, and thence to Manila, where she was sold as a slave. It so happened that the Viceroy of Mexico, the Marquis de Gelves, had written to the Governor of Manila that he wanted to buy a pretty little Chinese slave-girl for his household; so Catarina was sent to Acapulco in the Manila Galleon, or *Náo de China*,[2] dressed as a boy in order to preserve her from the undesirable attentions of sex-starved sailors on the seven or eight months' voyage across the Pacific.

The galleon reached Mexico at a time when the Viceroy had lost his job as the result of the celebrated riots of January 1624; but Catarina was purchased by a charitable and childless couple at Puebla de los Angeles, who wanted to bring her up as their daughter. Freed by her owners in their last wills and testaments, she then became the servant of a local priest who wished her to marry a Chinese slave of his, named Domingo Suarez. Being determined to preserve her much cherished virginity—even as a small child she preferred to play with poisonous snakes rather than with boys of

[1] Thomas Gage, *The English American* (ed. J. E. S. Thompson, University of Oklahoma Press, 1958), pp. 189–91.

[2] The Spaniards in Mexico had the confusing habit of calling all Orientals *Chinos*, whether they were Filipinos, Japanese, Indonesians, Indochinese, Indians or really Chinese. She was also described in her marriage registry as 'China, India, natural de la India'. To such an absurd length did the Spaniards carry this confusing nomenclature, that a seventeenth-century diarist in Mexico City habitually referred to the Philippines as *China*, noting that whenever a new Governor went to Manila, it was in his capacity as 'Governor of China' (*Licenciado* Don Antonio de Robles, *Diario de Sucesos Notables, 1665–1703* [alias 1665–1688] 2 vols., Mexico, 1853), *passim*.

her own age—she declined to marry her ardent suitor, unless Domingo would promise not to exercise his marital rights. Since her Spanish was so bad, Domingo did not understand her properly, and he accordingly agreed. When he subsequently tried to consummate the marriage, she would not let him do so; and although he was physically a very strong man, he miraculously became impotent every time he got into her bed. Later, he was prevented from approaching her by angels and by a crucifix placed between the two beds. Domingo was understandably very upset about this, and he accused her of being a witch; but Catarina bore him no malice. Being an excellent needlewoman and cook, she was able to make enough money to buy his freedom and set him up in business (in which he was not very successful, going bankrupt before his death).

Left a widow, and independent after the death of her priestly master, she lived a very devout and holy life in great poverty and squalor, giving away in charity all the money she earned as a seamstress and a cook. She also had the most remarkable series of visions and dreams, claiming that she visited in spirit all the courts and battlefields of Europe, and the pagan capitals of China and Japan. She prophesied the imminent conversion of that island-empire to Christianity, and she declared that Charles II of Spain would have many healthy and flourishing children. She alleged that she frequently went up to Heaven and down to Purgatory and to Hell, and that God and the Virgin Mary constantly quarrelled over who would do her the greatest spiritual favours. Her prayerful intercession saved the *flota* of 1678 in a most dangerous storm, and she was similarly responsible for one of the few victories which the Spaniards won against the Buccaneers at this time, when Pedro de Castro drove them from La Laguna de Terminios near Campeche. She saved the outward-bound *flota* in 1687 in another storm, and accompanied it on its return to Spain in her last miraculous manifestation. A tireless spiritual world-traveller, she was able to give her confessors, 'of whom she had many', the most convincing and detailed descriptions of all the places and peoples she visited. Last, not least, she spent nearly all her waking time in prayer and meditation, displaying the profoundest veneration for the sacerdotal office by going down on her hands and knees and kissing the footprints of any priest who passed by her hovel.[1]

[1] Alonso Ramos, S.J., *Primera [y Segunda] Parte de los prodigios de la Omnipotencia y milagros de la Gracia en la vida de la venerable sierva de Dios*

This was, of course, an age when the miraculous was accepted as commonplace, and when no good Roman Catholic Christian doubted that God and the Virgin Mary and the Saints could and would intervene in daily life. Even so, it is rather surprising that this illiterate woman was able to achieve and retain the fame of being to all intents and purposes a saint. Not only her two ecclesiastical biographers believed this, but a whole array of the most prominent people in Mexico, including the Viceroy Don Gaspar de Sandoval, Conde de Galve (1688–95), the Archbishop of Puebla de Los Angeles, and numerous theologians and superiors of the Religious Orders. Even the Inquisition did not at first object to the publication of such sweeping claims; although a few years later it did order the suppression of the Jesuit Padre Alonso Ramos' massive and hagiographical biography on the grounds that the book contained 'useless and improbable revelations, visions, and apparitions'.[1] This belated condemnation by the Inquisition ensured that *La China Poblana* would not become a saint in the same way as her contemporary, Mariana de Paredes y Flores, 'the Lily of Quito', (1619–45), who was canonised by the Ecuadorian populace in her lifetime and by Pope Pius XII in 1950.[2] Ironically enough, Catarina

---

Catharina de San Joan, natural del Gran Mogor, difunta en esta imperial Ciudad de la Puebla de los Angeles (2 vols., Puebla, 1689, Mexico, 1690); Joseph de El Castillo Graxeda, *Compendio de la vida y virtudes de la Venerable Catharina de San Juan* (Puebla de los Angeles, 1692). Both Ramos and Graxeda had been her confessors. Her biographers are confused and contradictory about her age, stating that she was 'about 88 years old' when she died in 1688, but that she had come to Acapulco as a child of 'ten, eleven, or thirteen years old', in the Manila galleon of 1624.

[1] Cf. the article in the *Dicionario Porrua* (ed. 1966), *in voce* Catarina de San Juan. I have not been able to see R. Carrasco Puente, *Bibliografía de Catarina de San Juan y de la China Poblana*, Mexico, 1950. Readers of Norman Douglas, *Old Calabria* (ed. John Davenport, Penguin Books, 1962), will find chapters 10, 'The Flying Monk', and 31, 'Southern Saintliness', reminiscent of the miracles ascribed to *La China Poblana*, as pointed out to me by Mr. John Bury. My friend and colleague, Professor K. Enoki of Tokyo University has also published an article in Japanese, 'Mekishiko *ryūgū* no Ajiya fujin China Poblana no koto', in *Historical Essays in Honour of Dr Noboru Orui's 77th Birthday* (also in Japanese), Tokyo, 1962.

[2] John Leddy Phelan, *The Kingdom of Quito in the Seventeenth Century: Bureaucratic Politics in the Spanish Empire* (University of Wisconsin Press, 1967), pp. 190–5; Frances Parkinson Keyes, *The Rose and the Lily* (New York, 1961). The Rose of Mrs. Parkinson Keyes is, of course, Santa Rosa of Lima

de San Juan attained a posthumous and lasting fame in a way that her biographers never intended. Although she herself always dressed in the oldest, raggedest and plainest garments she could find, the name *China Poblana* was given to a type of woman's dress at Puebla which came to be the hallmark of ladies whose reputation for chastity was none of the best, as Fanny Calderón de la Barca, the Scottish-American wife of the Spanish Minister to Mexico, discovered to her embarrassment in 1840.[1]

Coming southwards to the viceroyalty of Peru, which theoretically comprised the whole of South America save for Brazil and the 'Wild Coast' of the Guyanas in the sixteenth and seventeenth centuries, the role of the pioneer Spanish woman in Peru has been admirably analysed by James Lockhart in his previously quoted *Spanish Peru, 1532–63*. Much of what he says about them is applicable to the rest of the colonial period, and, in a greater or lesser degree, to other regions of colonial Spanish America as well. One of the points which he makes is that the *encomenderos'* wives were the most important and influential women in Peru, their position in its way being as central as that of their husbands. They were the heads of large households of dependents, servants and slaves. Widowhood usually ended in early remarriage, since unmarried women and widows were legally not supposed to be allowed to be heads of *encomiendas*, and all the social pressures operated to make a widow take a second husband. Consequently, one woman might retain the same house, servant staff, *encomienda* and landed property through three or four husbands. These women were liable to become wealthier with each husband they took, and they often had

---

(1586–1617). Like the 'Lily of Quito' (1618–45), Catarina de San Juan steadfastly refused all offers to enter a local convent, although she remained on good terms with the nuns, perhaps feeling that life in the well-endowed nunneries of Mexico was not austere enought for her continual mortifications of the flesh. For a nun who was a similar trans-Atlantic spiritual traveller and also practised singular mortifications of the flesh, see T. D. Kendrick, *Mary of Agreda: The Life and Legend of a Spanish Nun* (London 1967). An equally celebrated *beata* in Guatemala was D. Anna Guerra de Jesús (1639–1713), whose life was likewise written by one of her Jesuit confessors: Antonio de Siria, S.J., *Vida Admirable y prodigiosas virtudes de la venerable Sierva de Dios D. Anna Guerra de Jesus* (Guatemala, 1716).

[1] Fanny Calderón de la Barca, *Life in Mexico* (2 vols. Boston 1843), Letter the Ninth, pp. 88–9; Howard T. Fisher and Marion Hall Fisher (eds.) *Life in Mexico. The Letters of Fanny Calderón de la Barca, with new material from the author's private journals* (New York, 1966), pp. 82–4, 118–19, 125–6, 276.

the reputation, whether deserved or not, of being more heartless, avaricious, and exploitive of their *encomienda* Amerindians and slaves than were their menfolk.[1] Some of these widows might 'drag their feet' a bit before remarrying, despite the insistence of the vice-regal authorities that they should do so as soon as possible. Lockhart cites the record for non-compliance in sixteenth-century Peru as set by Maria de Escobar, a woman of immense wealth, seniority and political power, who managed to place a three-year interval between her second and third husbands. But her record was easily surpassed in seventeenth-century Chile by Doña Catalina de los Rios de Lisperguer, who only married once but continued to hang on to her three *encomiendas* for her lifetime.

This remarkable woman, born in Santiago de Chile about 1604–5, was descended from two Germans, one of them a page of the Emperor Charles V and the other a companion of the pioneer *conquistador*, Valdivia, and who had a *mestiza* daughter by a local Amerindian 'princess'. She also had Castilian blood in her veins, and she inherited a tendency to sadistic violence from her parents on both sides. Her mother, Doña Catalina Lisperguer, tried to poison the Governor of Chile, Alonso de Rivera, and she flogged to death a natural daughter of her husband. Her paternal grandfather, Gonzalo de los Rios, made his Amerindians give false evidence against an innocent man, leading to the latter's execution. Her grandmother, Maria de Encio Sarmiento, killed her own husband and made her Amerindians (?or her Negroes) do diabolical dances in the intervals of flogging them. When someone remonstrated with her over this, she retorted that even if St Francis came down from Heaven and told her to stop this diversion, she would not do so. Her great-grandfather, Bartolomé Flores (*alias* Blumenthal) was accused of poisoning one of his own daughters and of promoting various injustices. However, all these family excesses, and others too numerous to mention here, were surpassed by the sadistic cruelty of Doña Catalina de los Rios Lisperguer, or *La Quintrala* as she was called, a term of uncertain origin.[2]

[1] J. Lockhart, *Spanish Peru, 1532–1563* (1968), pp. 156–8. For a recent discussion on the thorny question of the origin and development of the *encomienda* see his article in *Hispanic-American Historical Review*, vol. 49.

[2] The basic work is still that first published in 1877 by Benjamin Vicuña Mackenna, *Los Lisperguer y La Quintrala (Doña Catalina de los Rios): Episodio histórico social con numerosos documentos inéditos*, of which there are improved and corrected editions, in 1908, and by Jaime Eyzaguirre, Santiago de Chile,

Her victims included her own father, and one of her lovers, Don Enrique Enriques de Guzmán, a knight of the Order of St. John of Jerusalem, who was killed by one of her Negro slaves at her orders. She then allowed the slave to expiate his crime on the gallows, after having promised to save him. She also killed forty Amerindians and slaves of her own household and *encomiendas*, many of whom were tortured to death with singular barbarity. Most of these crimes were perpetrated on her *encomienda* of La Ligua, where she was already denounced by the Bishop of Santiago in 1634, for 'committing great cruelties on her servants and slaves'. Although such denunciations were well evidenced and frequently repeated, she was not called to answer for them until twenty-six years later, when the *Oidor*, Dr Juan de Huerta Gutiérrez, visited her estates to take the evidence of her employees against her. His investigation, carried out in June 1660, disclosed a horrifying state of affairs, as can be seen from the following typical passages in his detailed and documented report:[1]

'Doña Catalina used to punish every day, as she has done for many years past, and sometimes two or three times, all the people in her service, great and small, married and unmarried female Indians, stripping them stark naked, tying them to stakes or ladders with their hands above their heads, or suspending them head downwards, or with their hands tied, and laid out on the ground; they were beaten until they bled and choked profusely, and by her Negroes, Julian and Lorenzo. These victims included Juan, Ignacio, Augustín, Jordanillo, Indians, and others. And after they had been flogged in this way, she had their bodies washed with cold water, and sometimes with salt, chiles and urine. She then had them flogged and washed again in the same way, so that this mistreatment was virtually continuous, by day and night. It often happened that a single individual was flogged three or four times in a single day, with which the wounds on their bodies were multiplied.

1950. Cf. also the short but suggestive essay by Joaquin Edwards Belo, *La Quintrala, Portales, y algo más* (Santiago de Chile, 1969). La Quintrala married in 1631 and her husband died in 1650.

[1] First published in full by Domingo Amuñátegui Solar, *Las Encomiendas de indígenas en Chile*, vol. II (Santiago de Chile, 1910), pp. 121–60, 159–79, 'Delitos cometidos por doña Catalina de los Rios i Lisperguer; esposicion del Oidor Huerta Gutierrez en 1660', whence the extracts in Jaime Eyzaguirre, op. cit.

'The instrument used for flogging them was usually a leather strap, or rods of quince-wood and sometimes stinging-nettles, as happened to Rufina, a Negress, and to Pascual, a Mulato, plunging them afterwards into cold water, so as to increase their pain, or beating them with green thorns, as happened to Pablo Yane, to the Negro Julian, and to other persons. They were likewise given in the course of the day many blows with sticks; she pinched them and then struck them with stones on the face and head. After being flogged, they were often burnt with pitch, lighted candles, and fire-brands. And at many other times they were held suspended over a fire with four persons holding their hands and feet. And on one occasion, when she had flogged the Mulata, Herrera, she had her suspended head downwards in a basin of live coals and chiles, from which she very nearly died of suffocation.

'She also used to burn their mouths with [boiling] milk, eggs, and live coals, putting these inside and closing their lips. She hurt their eyes by putting chiles in them, pinching them, and slapping them with stinging-nettles.'

Even though convicted of having murdered thirty-nine persons in this way (to which she subsequently added a fortieth, a wretched Mulata girl), nothing much happened to 'La Quintrala'. She had to leave her estates and remain under house-arrest at Santiago, pending the result of her appeal. But when she died in January 1665, she was buried in state in the local Augustinian church, to which she had been a generous benefactress in life and under the terms of her will, dressed in the habit of a nun. Not surprisingly, her evil deeds persisted in the popular memory. Servants in nineteenth-century Santiago still refused to spend the night in the house which they believed (apparently erroneously) to have been hers, and which she was supposed to haunt.

Her husband had died in 1650 and her only male child predeceased her; but she was able to evade being brought to trial for her crimes and to retain her *encomiendas* (for she had more than one) for so long, because she had several relatives by marriage among successive judges of the local *Audiencia* or High Court. The Crown had forbidden *Oidores* and magistrates to marry Creole ladies within the areas of their jurisdiction; but this rule, though often reiterated, was as often and increasingly evaded. The case of

La Quintrala may have been one of the worst miscarriages of justice, all the more flagrant because the Bishop had denounced her repeatedly, and bishops were not to be sneezed at in colonial Spanish America; but there were many other equally irregular if less tragic cases. Professor Phelan has documented the impunity with which Dr Antonio de Morga, a former upright judge in the Philippines, broke all the rules in the book during his scandalous career as *Oidor* of Quito, nor would it be difficult to find many other examples.[1] I will only instance Dr Alonso Maldonado de Torres, who married a wealthy Creole widow in 1608, when he was President of the Audiencia of La Plata (Chuquisaca, or Charcas) in High Peru. He had the tact to soften this breach of the rules by pointing out to the Crown that his bride had lent 50,000 ducats' worth of silver bars to the Royal Exchequer free of interest, and might well do so again. The Crown evidently took the hint, as he was promoted to Councillor of the Indies after his return to Spain, the highest post to which a professional lawyer could aspire.[2] Creole ladies of good family were usually keen to marry judges, as La Quintrala's sister had done. This gave them equal (or better) social status than the wives of *encomenderos,* and it afforded all kinds of opportunities of using their husband's influence to help their families and their children.

It would, obviously, be absurd and unfair to conclude that the Spanish and Creole woman of Peru were only concerned with their own status, prosperity, or prestige, and indifferent to the public weal. The history of the Conquest, whether in Mexico, Peru, or elsewhere is full of examples of women who fought alongside and encouraged their menfolk, nursed the sick and wounded, and displayed a spirit of exemplary self-sacrifice. Nor are such attitudes absent in later periods. In a *cédula real* addressed to the citizens of Arequipa on 19 September 1580, Philip II expresses his gratitude for the way in which they, and more especially their wives, had answered his appeal for a voluntary contribution to meet the vast expenses of his wars against Turks, infidels, and heretics in Europe

[1] John Phelan, *The Kingdom of Quito in the seventeenth century* (1967), pp. 147–207.

[2] Alonso Maldonado de Torres, *Oidor* of Lima, 1585–1602; President of the Audiencia of La Plata (Chuquisaca), 1602–11; Councillor of the Indies at Madrid, 1612 to 1628, when he died. For his marriage, see José Vazquez Machicado, *Catalogo de documentos referentes a Potosí en el Archivo de Indias de Sevilla* (Potosí, 1964), pp. xxi, 19–24.

(and, he might have added, the conquest of Catholic Portugal, which he had just completed). He extolled the ladies of Arequipa for not only giving money, but their personal jewelry and gold ornaments, 'just as the Roman matrons did for the defence of their Republic', assuring them that he and his descendants would never forget such generosity.[1]

At a slightly later date, when the English corsair, Sir Richard Hawkins, was cruising off the coast of Peru and had repulsed a preliminary attempt by a small Spanish squadron fitted out at Callao to take his ship, the *Dainty*, when the defeated Spaniards returned to port and went ashore: 'They were so mocked and scorned by the women, as scarce anyone, by day would show his face. They reviled them with the name of cowards and chickens, and craved licence from the Viceroy, to be admitted in their rooms and to undertake the surrender of the English ship. I have been certified for truth, that some of them affronted their soldiers with daggers and pistols by their sides. This wrought such effects in the hearts of the disgraced, as they vowed either to recover their reputation lost, or to follow us unto England.' Two ships and a pinnace were therefore promptly refitted for a second attack on the *Dainty*, which this time was successful.[2]

Apart from the heroines—and viragoes—in the conquest of Mexico and Peru, whose feats have been well publicised, such as those of Inéz Suárez, mistress of Pedro de Valdivia, pioneer but ill-fated *conquistador* of Chile, there were many others who were involved in the later frontier wars against unsubdued Amerindian tribes from the Chichemecas of Northern Mexico to the Araucanians of Southern Chile. It has been observed with, I think, good reason, that whereas there were a fair number of male Spaniards who deserted to the enemy, or voluntarily 'went native' after being captured by them, and subsequently refused to return to white civilisation, the captured Spanish and Creole women behaved very differently. There is apparently no recorded instance of one having become a voluntary renegade. Those who were captured by the Amerindians and raped by them, sometimes made their escape years

---

[1] *Cédula* dated Badajoz, 19 September 1580, certified by the Public Notary and Secretary of the Cabildo of Arequipa, Gaspar Hernández in 1581 (writer's collection).

[2] *The Observations of Sir Richard Hawkins, Knight* (1622), ed. J. A. Williamson, Argonaut Press, 1933, p. 118.

4

later with their half-Indian children. Others refused to do so when they had the opportunity, from a mixture of wounded pride and shame (*pundonor*) which induced them to remain where they were rather than rejoin their own kith and kin.[1]

The Spanish woman's sense of *pundonor* was, if anything, even stronger than that of the man. A Jesuit priest with long experience of ministering to criminals and dissidents in the prisons and the Inquisition of sixteenth- and seventeenth-century Seville, noted in 1610: 'One thing that I have observed over a long period of time, is that of twenty women who are tortured, eighteen of them never confess their offence. And if they are stripped to the waist in order that they should be tortured for not confessing their crime, there is no chance whatever of getting them to confess, because having suffered what is worse to them than any physical torture, which is being stripped, they will endure what is less to them [i.e. the physical pain].'[2]

I may add that just as the Spaniards' attitudes to the various Amerindian races and tribes which they encountered varied a good deal, so did the response of the Amerindians to them. Considering the way that the traditionally brutal and licentious soldiery, let alone the sex-starved *conquistadores*, behaved to the Amerindian women, whether willing or unwilling, whom they captured, it is not surprising that the Araucanians, for instance, behaved likewise when they had the chance. But not all the tribes did so, even when they were hostile. An anonymous description of Paraguay compiled about 1612 stated that the Guaycurú tribe of the Gran Chaco had been fighting the Spaniards of Asunción for about sixty years. 'During the heat of battle they are very cruel and give quarter to none; but when the fight is over, they never harm their prisoners, and least of all the women, whom they let alone until they marry of their own accord. The children whom they capture, they bring up in their manners and customs.' Another account of 1643 stated that the Spaniards still 'stood in awe of them, as these Indians are very warlike, and wrought continual havoc, stealing cattle, destroying

---

[1] Cf. Alberto Salas, 'Naufragos, prisioneros y renegados y la conquista de America', in *Imago Mundi. Revista de la Historia de la Cultura*, no. 7 (Buenos Aires, 1955), pp. 54–9.

[2] 'Compendio' of Padre Pedro León, S.J. 1578–1618, *apud* Antonio Domínguez Ortiz, *Crisis y Decadencia de la España de los Austrias* (Barcelona, 1969), p. 68.

farms and crops, carrying off European women, including a sister of the finest governor who was ever in Paraguay, Hernandarias de Saavedra.'[1]

A lecture of this brevity, which has to cover a continent in space and three centuries in time, does not, obviously, allow me to analyse in depth many of the problems concerned with Iberian women in the New World. But before glancing at the Portuguese in Brazil, I may mention some aspects, which might well repay future research, and about which there must be plenty of archival material. Prostitution, sometimes described as the world's oldest profession, naturally existed in the New, long before the arrival of the Spaniards. Spanish civilisation being essentially urban, and prostitution an urban more than a rural activity, we naturally find it installed at an early date. Exactly how early I cannot say, but a *cédula real* of 4 August 1526 authorised a certain Bartolomé Conejo to build in Puerto Rico 'a house for public women ... in a suitable place, because there is need for it in order to avoid other [worse] harms'— an excuse commonly alleged in the legislature of the time. In the same year, one Juan Sánchez Sarmiento was authorised by the Crown to open a brothel in Santo Domingo.[2]

Brothels doubtless existed elsewhere especially in the rich mining-camp or township, the Villa Imperial de Potosí, which possessed (at one time) the largest population in the New World. Potosí was a magnet for miners and adventurers of every description, and it naturally attracted ladies of easy virtue as well. However, as Lockhart has pointed out, there was nothing like a mass demand for Spanish prostitutes, and most of these women operated on an individual basis. 'Spanish men found Indian women attractive, and any Spaniard could have as many as he wanted. Spanish prostitutes catered more to the need of Spaniards to be near a woman who shared their language and culture. As much as anything else they were entertainers, who might, like María de Ledesma in Potosí have a fine *vihuela* or guitar and know how to play and sing well. Jokingly, half in derision, these women were commonly called

---

[1] C. R. Boxer, *Salvador de Sá and the struggle for Brazil and Angola, 1602–1686* (London, 1952), pp. 90–1. Hernandarias de Saavedra was Governor of Paraguay, 1601–8 and 1614–17.

[2] José María Ots, *Instituciones Sociales* (1934), p. 254. It is not stated whether the inmates were Spanish, Amerindian, or *mestiza* women.

doña by their clients . . . but they were not so termed in any serious context.'[1]

True enough, but I would add that many Spaniards did *not* find the Amerindian women particularly attractive, preferring Mulatas and Mestizas, of whom the former more especially provoked frequent denunciations from pillars of church and state. Thomas Gage in his inimitable account of Mexico City as he saw it in 1624, wrote: 'Both men and women are excessive in their apparel, using more silks than stuffs and cloth. Precious stones and pearls further much their vain ostentation—nay a blackamoor or tawny young maid and slave will make hard shift but she will be in fashion with her neck-chain and bracelets of pearls, and her ear-bobs of some considerable jewels. The attire of this baser sort of people of blackamoors and mulattoes (which are of a mixed nature, of Spaniards and blackamoors) is so light, and their carriage so enticing, that many Spaniards even of the better sort (who are too prone to venery) disdain their wives for them.' After a whole page of very detailed description of the dress of these enchanting and enticing Mulatas, our Dominican friar adds: 'Most of these are or have been slaves, though love have set them loose at liberty to enslave souls to sin and Satan . . . such jet-like damsels . . . who with their bravery and white mantles seem to be, as the Spaniard saith, *mosca en leche*, a fly in milk.'[2] However unedifying, a history of prostitution in colonial Spanish America might repay investigation and be worth writing.

On a more elevated level, it would be interesting to compare the position of the married Spanish or Creole lady with that of her Anglo-Saxon equivalents. It is commonly assumed that the latter had every advantage over the former, but I think his assumption may be largely or even entirely erroneous. From the works of José María Ots Capdequí, Professor Brading and others, we know that the legal position of women, and above all of widows, in the Spanish-American world was in some ways stronger than that of their Anglo-Saxon counterparts. Colonial Spanish America was governed by the inheritance laws of Castile. These laid down that all capital acquired during a marriage belonged equally to both partners, so that at the death of either spouse, the survivor was only entitled to half the estate. The deceased person's share was then

[1] James Lockhart, *Spanish Peru, 1532–63* (1969), pp. 161–2.
[2] Thomas Gage, *The English American* (ed. S. E. J. Thompson, 1958), pp. 68–9.

divided in equal portions among all the children of the marriage, male and female alike. The same fate awaited the survivor's half of the estate.[1] There were, of course, exceptions, such as the *mayorazgo*, or entailed estate, although even this did not necessarily descend in the male line and could, under certain circumstances, devolve on the females. But since primogeniture was not the general rule, as it was with the English landed gentry, Spanish girls might often be better off than English spinsters. It would, I think, be interesting to compare in this respect the position of the ladies of New England with those of New Spain.

Whatever might emerge from such a comparison, it is fairly safe to assert that Spanish-American women in the colonial period had, on the whole, a more enviable position than that of their Luso-Brazilian contemporaries. Granting with Hilaire Belloc that all generalisations are false including this one, the fact remains that a great cloud of witnesses testify to the rigorous seclusion in which the better class women were kept, from Jan Huighen van Linschoten in sixteenth-century Goa to Maria Graham in nineteenth-century Bahia. This attitude did not help to enliven family life in colonial Brazil, which the great Brazilian historian, Capistrano de Abreu, characterised as being 'taciturn father, obedient wife, cowed children'. As noted previously, their Spanish neighbours made fun of the jealous seclusion in which the Portuguese kept—or strove to keep—their wives and daughters. The Portuguese themselves were certainly not ashamed of this, save for a few eccentrics like the legal luminary, Tomé Pinheiro da Veiga, whose *Fastigimia*, written in the early seventeenth century, is full of mordant criticism of his compatriots' habit of secluding their women, which he compares unfavourably with the far more liberal attitude of the Spaniards.[2]

The Spanish tradition of women in government (Isabella the Catholic in Spain, Margarida of Parma and the Infanta Isabella in the Low Countries, Margarida of Mantua in Portugal) does not seem to have had any parallel in Portugal, unless we except the regency of King John IV's widow from 1656 to 1662, and she, after all, was a Spanish lady born and bred, daughter of the Duke of

[1] D. A. Brading, *Miners and Merchants in Bourbon Mexico, 1763–1810* (Cambridge University Press, 1971), pp. 102–3.

[2] Tomé Pinheiro da Veiga, *Fastigimia, ou Fastos Geniaes tirados da tumba de Merlin* (ed. Porto, 1911). There is an edition, in some respects more satisfactory, in Spanish translation by Narciso Alonso Cortés (Valladolid, 1916).

Medina Sidonia. Whereas the Viceroys of Mexico and (to a lesser extent, perhaps, of Peru) usually had their wives with them, I cannot off-hand recall a single Governor-General or a Viceroy of Brazil who took his spouse across the Atlantic. Nor, so far as I can ascertain, was there any Brazilian equivalent of the attractive and flirtatious *Limeña*, so enthusiastically described by visitors to the eighteenth-century City of Kings.[1]

Some of you are probably familiar with the Indo-Brazilian woman of the colonial and early national period as portrayed in Gilberto Freyre's *Casa Grande e Senzala* (*The Masters and the Slaves*) and in many other works. Freyre's 'sprawling masterpiece' is certainly indispensable for the student of Brazil, but it is open to serious criticism on several counts, including its lack of any time dimension. As Lockhart has observed: 'The task of deciding what the primary time reference is in *The Masters and the Slaves* is exceedingly difficult; apparently the time is more than anything else the early nineteenth century, whether Freyre realised it or not. At any rate, one can deduce . . . that Freyre projected a late and idealised version of the 'plantation' back into the whole colonial period, totally ignoring and implicitly denying the long and dynamic evolution of the sugar-producing complex and accompanying population'.[2] Ann Pescatello has also warned us, rightly enough, that we cannot yet formulate a general thesis about females in Brazilian colonial society by classifying them—as has been done in the recent past—as good or bad, *dona* or *prostituta*. 'The woman's role varies considerably in northern and southern plantation society, in upper class urban society, among the middle sectors, and among the masses of peasant and proletariat wherein the *amazia* and partial family are so common. A regular matriarch emerges with vital social and economic prerogatives, especially if she is a widow.'[3]

It does seem likely that if women were going to be able to play an important role outside of their own home and family in a male-dominated society, such as colonial Brazil undoubtedly was, what-

[1] For the eighteenth-century Limeña see W. Schurz, *This New World*, pp. 313–16, and the sources there quoted; Guillermo Furlong S. J., *La Cultura Femenina en la época colonia* (Buenos Aires, 1951), pp. 57–79.

[2] James Lockhart, 'The social history of colonial Spanish America, evolution and potential', in *Latin-American Research Review*, vol. VII (Spring, 1972), pp. 12–13.

[3] Ann Pescatello, in *Hispanic American Historical Review*, May, 1972, pp. 354–5.

ever nuances and modifications historical research in progress may reveal, wealthy widows would stand the best chance of doing so. In this connection, one would like to know more about such historical but still shadowy figures as Dona Brites de Albuquerque, the long-lived widow of Duante Coelho, the first donatory or lord-proprietor of the captaincy of Pernambuco, of which she was called the *Governadora* ('Governess') after his death, and Maria da Cruz, a wealthy widow in the backlands of Bahia and Minas Gerais, who was one of the three ringleaders of the *motins do sertão* (rebellions in the backlands), in 1736–7.[1]

I mentioned previously that High Court Judges and senior magistrates in the viceroyalties of Mexico and Peru were not allowed to marry Creole ladies within the area of their jurisdiction unless they first obtained the permission of the Crown, but that, in fact, this rule was often broken. A similar rule obtained in the Portuguese colonial empire and here it seems to have been even more widely disregarded. The recent researches of Stuart Schwartz have shown that a constant process of absorption of Portuguese (and of Luso-Brazilian) judges into the upper levels of Brazilian society became an increasingly marked trend in the eighteenth century.[2] Incidentally, I may add that it was the *Paulista* wife of a returning Portuguese judge who was the heroine of the successful defence of the homeward-bound *Nossa Senhora do Carmo e Santo Elias,* which was attacked by three sail of Algerian corsairs off the bar of Lisbon in March 1714. History does not relate what part her lawyer-husband played in the two-day naval action; but Dona Rosa Maria de Siqueira not only acted as nurse to the wounded and encouraged the defenders by her voice and example, but for some time took the place of the master-gunner (*condestauel*) who was killed while aiming a cannon.[3]

Another exceptional lady of Paulista origin was Teresa Margarida da Silva e Orta (1711–1793), who wrote a political novel modelled on the *Télémaque* (1699) of Bishop de la Mothe-Fénelon. Her

[1] Maria da Cruz was arrested in 1737, but I have not been able to trace what subsequently became of her, nor of the part she actually played in the disturbances of 1736–7. Cf. *Revista do Archivo Publico Mineiro,* vol. 1 (Belo Horizonte 1896), pp. 661–8.

[2] B. Stuart Schwartz, 'Magistracy and Society in Colonial Brazil', in *Hispanic-American Historical Review,* vol. 50 (November 1970), pp. 715–30.

[3] For Dona Rosa Maria de Siqueira's amazonian conduct, cf. Aureliano Leite, *António de Albuquerque Coelho de Carvalho* (Lisboa, 1944), pp. 96–8.

Maximas de Virtude e Formosura was first published at Lisbon in 1752, and reissued in 1777 with the title of *Aventuras de Diófanes*. Like its French model, this work contains criticisms of the abuses to which absolute monarchs were liable, with suggestions on how they could be avoided. It does not advocate any liberalisation or democratisation of the government, but only an enlightened paternalism on the part of the Crown through a careful choice of competent and honest advisers. Teresa Margarida came to Portugal with her parents when she was only six years old; and she never returned to Brazil in the course of her long and agitated life. Her book probably owes something to her friend, Alexandre de Gusmão (1695–1753), the Brazilian-born private secretary of King John V, some of whose ideas it clearly reflects, and to whom it was ascribed on the title-page of a third edition published in 1790. Recent research has made it virtually certain that Teresa Margarida was, in fact, the real author of this work, the first of its kind in Luso-Brazilian literature.

One may presume that the Crown-lawyers who married Luso-Brazilian ladies chose their brides from those of them who were white, or could pass as such. Marriage with a coloured (or a Jewish-descended) woman in the seventeenth and eighteenth centuries would automatically have barred the husband and his descendants from holding office under the Crown, or from being a member of one of the three Portuguese Military Orders (Christ, Aviz, and Santiago), unless a special dispensation had been obtained. The same applied to candidates for the priesthood, all of whom had to prove that their parents and grandparents were each and every one of them, male and female, 'entire and legitimate Old Christians, of clean blood (*limpo sangue*), without any race of Jew, Moor [Muslim], Heretic, nor any other disallowed infected nation (*nem de outra infectã naçao reprovada*)'. Of course, in regions where white women were in very short supply, as they were in many parts of colonial Brazil, such instructions were not always enforced, but neither were they invariably a dead letter as is sometimes alleged.

The reservations of office for white men of 'pure' Old Christian blood likewise extended to the members of the municipal councils and to those of the tertiary or third Orders, as also to the charitable lay-order of the Misericórdia, to which reference has already been made (p. 33). Here again, the degree of enforcement of the clause concerning racial purity naturally varied with time and place, but the point I wish to make now is that the candidate's wife had to have the same qualifications, at any rate in theory and often enough in practice. Russell-Wood has given some interesting examples of this rule from Bahia, where the two successive husbands of Joana Leal, a locally born girl, were refused entry to the brotherhood of the Misericórdia on the grounds of the alleged impurity of her blood. Only after extensive and official enquiries had traced her grandparents back to the village of Luzã near Coimbra, and secured a written testimonial from the Secretary of the local Misericórdia that they had all been of pure blood, was the second husband finally admitted in 1680.[1]

I may add that the prejudice against Jewish and against Negro blood (*mulatice*) was much stronger than that against Amerindian or against white heretic blood. Some of the early settlers of good family mated (rather than married) with Amerindian 'princesses', as tribal chiefs' daughters were sometimes grandiloquently termed, and their descendants such as the Arco-Verdes in Pernambuco found this nothing to be ashamed of, nor did it disadvantage them socially. But 'New Christian' blood was a very different matter; and the taint of *mulatice* was even more difficult to expunge, although examples certainly exist where this was done in all the regions of Brazil. Pedro Taques, the fanatical genealogist of eighteenth-century São Paulo, cites the case of a rich Mulata girl who married a Portuguese military officer 'conquered by the handsome dowry'. Taques admitted that the children of this marriage were properly brought up and in due course married very well; but he did not fail to criticise Artur de Sá de Menezes, the Governor of Rio de Janeiro (1697-1702), for having acted as godfather to one of these Mulato children.[2]

The same racial prejudices existed in the nunneries of colonial Brazil, from the time that the first of these was founded at Salvador (Bahia) in 1678. The Poor Clares of the convent of Desterro became celebrated for their racial purity, their lavish way of life, the splendour of their religious services, and the sumptuous entertainments which they gave during the Lenten Carnival and on other occasions, which make the place sound more like a Bunny Club than an austerely religious institution. The entrance-requirement for

[1] John Russell-Wood, *Fidalgos and Philanthropists*, p. 137.
[2] Pedro Taques de Almeida Paes Leme, *Informação sobre as Minas de São Paulo* (ed. A. de E. Taunay, São Paulo, n.d.), pp. 43-4.

'purity of blood' was so well known that a Bahian father, whose daughters were slightly coloured, asked permission from the Crown to send them to Portugal, where their chances of admission to a convent would be better.[1] 'New Christian' blood, or even the suspicion of it, was likewise a grave handicap in most of colonial Brazil. Dona Ines Barreto de Albuquerque, a leading planter's wife in Pernambuco, who endowed a small hospital, Nossa Senhora do Paraizo and São Joao de Deus, at Recife in 1688, stipulated that the priest who would be placed in charge thereof must be 'an Old Christian, without there ever having been any rumour about him to the contrary; and if there is such a rumour among the public, then he shall not be appointed, even though he may be really an Old Christian.'[2] On the other hand, there are instances of persons of Jewish blood being admitted to the priesthood, due to deliberately false testimony given on oath by friends and relations. Crypto-Judaism in one form or another survived well into the eighteenth century in colonial Brazil, and it would be interesting to ascertain, from the Inquisition records relating to these cases, to what extent it was the women of the family who were responsible for its perpetuation rather than the men.[3]

If upper-class racially mixed marriages in Brazil were not so

[1] C. R. Boxer, *Portuguese Society in the Tropics, 1510–1800* (1965), pp. 92–5; J. Russell-Wood, *Fidalgos and Philanthropists*, pp. 58, 134, 178–9, 312, 321–2, and the sources there quoted. Susan Soeiro has in hand a well-documented Ph.D. thesis on the Desterro and its occupants, which will show another and more serious side to the social, financial, and intellectual aspects which were involved.

[2] 'Institutos do Hospital Invocação Nossa Senhora do Paraizo e São Joam de Deos, sito na Capitania de Pernambuco', original MS d. Recife, 21 Sept. 1688, with the autograph signatures of the co-founders, Dona Ines Barreto de Albuquerque and Dom Francisco de Sousa (writer's collection).

[3] An excellent and well documented preliminary survey of crypto-Judaism in colonial Brazil has been made by Arnold Wiznitzer, *Jews in Colonial Brazil* (Columbia University Press, 1960); see especially ch. vii, 'Late Brazilian Marranos, 1654–1722', pp. 143–67. The Lisbon Inquisition records relating to Jews and crypto-Jews in Brazil have also been used to good effect by José Goncalves Salvador, *Cristãos-Novos, Jesuitas e Inquisição. Aspectos da sua atuação nas capitanias do Sul, 1530–1680* (São Paulo, 1969) and by Anita Novinsky, *Cristãos Novos na Bahia, 1624–1654* (São Paulo, 1972), and in articles by Anita Novinsky and Sonia A. Sequeira, for which see *Revista de Historia*, 88 (São Paulo). See also the intriguing article by Helder Macedo, 'Menina e Moça e o problema de seu significado' in *Colóquio* (July 1972), pp. 21–31.

common as incautious readers of Gilberto Freyre may think, and if at certain times and places there were not many marriages at all,[1] the prevalence of miscegenation through concubinage in all classes of society is overwhelmingly attested. Even slave women had a good chance of bettering themselves in this way, and could earn their freedom in their master's bed, more particularly if he was unmarried. Russell-Wood cites one uxorious master, Pedro Domingues, who was consumed by jealousy at the thought of his concubine marrying. In his will of 1676, he granted her her freedom, the ownership of his house and three slaves, on the condition that she should stay single for the rest of her life.[2] This may have been rather an extreme case; but it was common enough for slave-owners who had children by their female slaves to make generous provision for both mother and child. It was, of course, far from uncommon for other owners to do nothing of the sort, and to make no special provision for any children they might have fathered or for the slave mother(s) concerned.

One gets the impression, but, let me hasten to add, only an impression, unfortified by any statistics, that the prostitution of slave-girls by their owners, whether male or female, was more common in Portuguese than in Spanish America. However that may have been, many owners depended for their livelihood on the daily or weekly earnings made by their slaves, whether in honest or dishonest ways. This was a widespread practice throughout the Portuguese world, not least in Lisbon itself. An English Capuchin friar who spent some months there in 1633, at a time when there were about 15,000 African slaves in the city out of a total population of some 150,000 souls, noted: 'These slaves are very profitable to their male and female owners. There are poor widows, ladies of quality, who have no other income and who live comfortably on the earnings of their male or female slave. This slave gets up very early in the morning, cleans the house, prepares the breakfast for the window, and then goes out to the waterfront or the market-place to buy something which he then sells by hawking from door to

---

[1] Only two marriages were celebrated in Bahia in 1738 among the better sort of people. Cf. Pedro Calmon, *Historia Social do Brasil, I, Espirito da Sociedade Colonial* (3rd ed., São Paulo, 1941), pp. 91–3. C. R. Boxer, *The Golden Age of Brazil, 1695–1750* (California University Press, 1962), pp. 164–6, 402–20, and the sources there quoted.

[2] J. Russell-Wood, *Fidalgos and Philanthropists, 1550–1755* (1968) p. 183.

door through the streets. In this way, the slave makes four *reales* a day, which is all for the widow, unless he has bargained with her previously to give her so much and keep the balance for himself.' Incidentally, the English Capuchin was greatly impressed by the physical fitness of the Negro slaves which he saw, declaring that 'most of them have handsomer and better proportioned bodies than the white men. A naked Negro looks better than a bare White.'[1] Whether widows were rich or poor, there can be no doubt that they could lead less cribbed, cabined and confined lives than those of respectable married women and their daughters. A glimpse of the latter category by a somewhat prejudiced but not dishonest pen, is available in the letters of Mrs Nathaniel Kindersley, a true blue Protestant housewife, who spent some weeks in the City of the Saviour at Bahia on her way to India in 1764:

'After what I have said of the general character of the men of this place, you will not expect to hear much in praise of the women; brought up in indolence, and their minds uncultivated, their natural quickness shows itself in cunning. As their male relations do not place any confidence in their virtue, they in return use their utmost art to elude the vigilance with which they are observed; and to speak the most favourably, a spirit of intrigue reigns among them. Were I to tell you what the darkness of evening conceals, amongst such as are not to be seen in the day but in a church, it would look like a libel on the sex.

'Many of them, when they are quite young, have delicate features and persons, but there is a certain yellow tint in their complexions which is disagreeable, and beside they look old very early in life.

'The dress is calculated for a hot climate; the best-dressed woman I have seen, had on a chintz petticoat, a flowered muslin shift, with deep ruffles, and a tucker of the same sewed upon it, without any stays or gown, but a large sash of crimson velvet, thrown round and round her waist. Her hair was braided behind, and fastened up with a great many combs; she had drops in her ears, and her hair was ornamented with a sort of egret, or rather

---

[1] British Museum, Sloane MS. 1572, fls. 61–2. This anonymous and untitled manuscript diary of a journey from Brussels through France, Spain and Portugal and return by sea from Lisbon was written in Spanish by an English Capuchin friar, whom I have not yet been able to identify.

a large lump of massive gold, embossed and set with diamonds; on her neck were several rows of small gold chain; and on her arms she had bracelets of gold of great thickness, and each of them wide enough for two. A pair of slippers like the sash, completed the dress.'[1]

Similar accounts by earlier and later visitors to colonial Brazil need to be taken with a pinch of salt, in so far as they allege that amorous intrigues in upper-class society were commonplace. All the reliable evidence points the other way. Those who really were ladies knew how to conduct themselves as such, Vilhena observed of the Bahianas some forty years later. Inevitably, exceptions did occur, and the turning-wheel of the foundling-hospital at Salvador received a fair number of unidentified white children of obviously good if illegitimate parentage. But the annual number of white and coloured foundlings at Bahia does not seem to have exceeded 100 out of a total population of some 115,000 souls.[2]

As indicated in the previous chapter, an analysis of the dowries, wills, and testaments made by the citizens of Salvador proves that owners often freed their slaves on their death, conditionally or unconditionally; and they often made bequests for the benefit of unmarried female servants and relations. As Russell-Wood has pointed out in this connection, anxiety for the preservation of class status was allied to an obsession with the maintenance of purity of blood. 'Members of an essentially male-dominated society were influenced by these two factors into adopting matrilineal attitudes when making their wills ... The seclusion of women in colonial times has been considered by historians as indicative of the insignificant position they enjoyed, but it seems likely that the womanhood of colonial Bahia was a good deal more influential than is generally recognised.'[3]

This is certainly a point which may well repay further investigation, although it will not be easy to ascertain how far Luso-Brazilian husbands relied on and confided in their wives when discussing

---

[1] *Letters from the island of Teneriffe, Brazil, the Cape of Good Hope, and the East Indies. By Mrs. Kindersley* (London, 1777), pp. 41–3, letter dated Salvador, August 1764.

[2] J. Russell-Wood, *Fidalgos and Philanthropists, 1550–1755* (1968), pp. 311–315.

[3] Ibid., pp. 183, 320–2.

anything outside immediate family and household concerns. Not only the prejudiced Mrs Nathaniel Kindersley, but even Roman Catholic prelates who took a Pauline view of females considered that Luso-Brazilian custom was unduly severe in secluding respectable women. The Archbishop of Bahia complained in 1751 that the local girls of good families could not be induced to attend lessons given in the Ursuline Convent, owing to the opposition of their parents. These latter, 'despite the continual complaints of prelates, missionaries, confessors and preachers, kept their daughters in such strict seclusion that they rarely let them go out to hear Mass, much less for any other reason'. The Archbishop added that this practice was not confined to white women, but was imitated by coloured girls, 'and by any others who can make confession at home'.[1] Small wonder if, under these circumstances, many aristocratic young ladies of Bahia preferred becoming Poor Clares in the well-endowed and relatively uninhibited Convent of the Desterro to either marriage or spinsterhood in a home of their own.

[1] C. R. Boxer, *The Golden Age of Brazil, 1695–1750* (1962) pp. 137–8. As stated in note 1, p. 58, a well-documented study of the Desterro Convent will be published by Susan Soeiro in due course, which may well revise many assumptions now held about it.

CHAPTER THREE

Portuguese Asia and the Spanish Philippines

The 'State of India' (*o Estado da India*), as the Portuguese called their string of coastal settlements, fortresses, and trading-posts (*feitorias*) between the Cape of Good Hope and Japan, stretched at its greatest extent from Sofala in South-east Africa to Macao in China. Since adequate coverage in time and space is impossible, I have chosen to concentrate on three main areas: Goa and the 'Province of the North' (*Provincia do Norte*) on the West coast of India; the *prazos* or entailed estates of Zambesia; and the City of the Name of God of Macao in China. This survey will be rounded off by a glance at the Spanish colonial society of Manila.

The first point to note is that although more Portuguese women and girls emigrated to Asia (the great majority to Goa) than went to West Africa, yet the numbers of those who went to the East were certainly far less than those who went to Brazil. It is true that we have no long runs of statistics for emigration to any of these regions to prove this point mathematically; but such a conclusion is inescapable to anyone who has examined the existing evidence carefully and impartially. Admittedly, an attempt to controvert this fact was made by the late Dr Germano da Silva Correia, in a voluminous work entitled *História da colonização portuguesa na India* (6 vols. Lisboa, 1948–56). This author deserves great credit for the ant-like industry with which he ransacked the archives at Lisbon and Goa to find material on feminine emigration from Portugal to Asia. Undeniably, he has produced much factual evidence with names and dates, to show that more Portuguese women did go out to 'Golden Goa' than most historians, including myself, had previously suspected. But his work (unindexed, alas) is vitiated by his preconception that there was an enormous current of feminine emigration from Portugal to India, particularly in the sixty years of the 'Spanish captivity' and the following war of the

63

Restoration with Spain (1580–1668).[1] Obsessed by this erroneous conviction, he interprets much of his own evidence arbitrarily (though perfectly honestly), and he often builds far-reaching and entirely erroneous deductions on some small piece of evidence which he had misunderstood. To take one example out of many, discussing the number of Portuguese women who allegedly came out to India in 1621, he lists a total of some forty-six names, of whom only three were actually embarked on the India-fleet of that year. The others, on the evidence of the documents which he prints, were either born in India, or else had come out in a previous year, usually at an unrecorded date. He has also failed to notice that of the twelve sail which left Lisbon for Goa that year only one ship reached its destination, the others being forced back by contrary winds and weather. Yet on the basis of these three girls who got to Goa in 1621 he writes '. . . 1621, one of the years of the seventeenth century, in which a greater number of orphans of the King and Luso-Iberian damsels came out and settled in India, besides innumerable families of the same ethnic and geographical origins who emigrated from Portugal in order to establish themselves in the great zones of Lusitanian settlement. We have thus proved, once again, in the most irrefutable way, that the Luso-feminine emigration, allegedly in decline, far from this, was in reality growing at an astonishing rate.' Yet he produces not a jot or a tittle of evidence to show that 'muitíssimas familias' emigrated to India in 1621, besides the three orphans whom he names.[2] His confident assertion, made, I reiterate, in perfect good faith, is based upon the totally un-unwarranted assumption that since three orphan girls left that year, 'very many families' must have done so. Dr da Silva Correia's monumental work, while extremely useful for the voluminous documentation which it does provide, must therefore be used with great caution. His deductions, more often than not, do not follow from the evidence which he presents.

We have seen (p. 27 above) that the Portuguese Crown, unlike the Castilian, tended to discourage women from going out to the

[1] Germano da Silva Correia, *História da Colonização Portuguesa na India*, vol. IV (Lisboa, 1960), pp. 15, 64–5 (where he argues that over a million persons of both sexes 'in the flower of their youth' must have left Portugal for India in 1580–1640), 93–4, and elsewhere. There would not have been standing room in the available shipping for such absurdly inflated numbers.

[2] Germano da Silva Correia, *História da Colonização*, vol. III, pp. 340–71, especially pp. 369–70.

Asian and African 'conquests' (*conquistas*, as these colonies were most commonly termed for centuries). Save for fleeting instances, it never passed legislation ordering husbands to cohabit with their wives on one or the other side of the ocean, as the Castilian Crown so often (if so ineffectively) did. I am not sure of the reasons for this striking difference in the attitude of the two Crowns, but perhaps the expense and dangers of the long six to eight months' voyage from Lisbon to Goa had something to do with it. The average male emigrant to the East could not have afforded to take his wife and/or daughters to India, without a monetary grant (*ajuda de custo*) from the Crown. The impecunious Portuguese monarchs neither would nor could grant these on a lavish scale. It has also been a tradition for centuries in Portugal that the man usually emigrates alone, even to places as relatively close as Brazil, or nowadays, to France and West Germany, though there are signs within the last few years of this changing at last.[1] In any event, whatever the reasons, the number of Portuguese women emigrating to the East was very low in comparison with that of the men, despite Dr da Silva Correia's claims to the contrary. It is significant that whereas the viceroys of Mexico usually had their wives with them, at any rate in the seventeenth and eighteenth centuries, no wife of a Portuguese viceroy or governor-general of India accompanied her husband to Goa between 1549 and 1750. When the Marchioness of Tavora insisted on sailing to Goa with her husband in 1750, this caused a great sensation at Lisbon and the King only reluctantly gave her the required leave to do so. There are instances of magistrates and other government officials, as well as of private individuals, such as the famous physician Garcia d'Orta, taking their wives or female relatives with them, or sending for them later; but they are much

---

[1] Gastão de Sousa Dias, a competent historian with long experience of the Portuguese Congo and Angola, noted in 1927: 'The man emigrates alone. The result is that he becomes unhappy overseas and feels out of place when he eventually returns to Portugal, where he finds everything changed. The Portuguese woman does not accompany him, and, for this reason, the possibilities of our controlling this gigantic Africa diminish daily...' Germano Da Silva Correia, op. cit., vol. v, p. 496). Feminine emigration to Angola increased after the Second World War, although not to the extent that Salazar's government desired and tried to foster with its development schemes. For the women left behind in Portugal, see Colette Callier, 'Soajo, une Communauté feminine rurale de l'Alto-Minho', *Bulletin des Études Portugaises*, Tome 27 (Lisboa–Paris, 1966), pp. 237–78, especially pp. 253, 264, 268–9.

rarer than the corresponding Spanish-American examples.[1] In the vast majority of cases, only sons accompanied their fathers to India, as can be seen from the surviving if fragmentary records of passengers in the Indiamen.

The chief exception to this rule of officially discouraging female emigration from Portugal to the East lies in the so-called 'Orphans of the King' (*Orfãas del Rei*), whose numbers Dr Germano da Silva Correia has investigated so diligently, if often so uncritically. These, as their name implies, were orphan girls of marriageable age, who were sent out in annual batches from orphanages at Lisbon and Oporto (and very occasionally from a few other places such as Coimbra) at the expense of the Crown. They were usually provided with dowries in the form of minor government posts, or with small grants of land, for the men who might marry them after their arrival at Goa. The first contingent left Lisbon in 1545 and the system apparently continued to function intermittently until the eighteenth century. So far as I can ascertain from the names and numbers given by Dr Germano da Silva Correia, the largest number embarked for India in any given year was fifty-four in 1560; although, as noted above, he makes unsubstantiated claims for hundreds of women embarking in some years. But from his own statistics, it is safer to deduce that the number of fifty-four was exceptionally high, and that something between five and fifteen would have been a more likely annual figure. In some years none were sent at all, although Francisco Rodrigues da Silveira, who served in India from 1585 to 1598, was clearly exaggerating when he wrote 'It shows in truth great negligence on our part that we send every year to India four or five great ships laden with men, but carrying no women whatever.'[2] It is true that the Crown temporarily stopped the dispatch of these girls in 1595, but it soon revived the practice, although never on a scale sufficiently large to make any appreciable contribution to the establishment of a large 'white'

---

[1] Elaine Sanceau, 'Una familia portuguesa quinhentista na India . . . carta de Maria Pinheiro, viuva do Dr Francisco de Mariz', *Studia*, vol. 1 (Lisboa, 1958), pp. 101–10. Augusto da Silva Carvalho, *Garcia d'Orta* (Coimbra, 1934), especially pp. 32–41.

[2] Extracts from Francisco Rodrigues da Silveira's original MS. in the British Museum (Add. MSS. 25419), which I have consulted in the original, were published by A. de S. S. Costa Lobo under the title of *Memorias de um soldado da India, 1585–98* (Lisboa, 1877).

population in Portuguese Asia, which never existed outside the imagination of Dr da Silva Correia.[1]

It can be estimated with some degree of accuracy that during the sixteenth century approximately 4,000 people left Portugal yearly for overseas, the majority of them being able-bodied and unmarried young men, bound for 'Golden Goa' and further east, relatively few of whom ever returned to Europe. An outward-bound Indiaman which carried 800 or more men would only have some ten or fifteen women aboard and often none at all. During the seventeenth and eighteenth centuries, the numbers of men emigrating to India fell off noticeably after 1630, as can be seen from the statistics of outward-bound shipping. Whereas in the decade 1620–29, some 67 Indiamen left Lisbon for Goa, this number fell abruptly to 30 in the decade 1630–40, and it never recovered appreciably thereafter. Moreover, whereas the number of voluntary emigrants to India continued to decrease, owing to the vastly superior attractions of Brazil for the surplus population of Portugal and the Atlantic Islands, the relative proportion of *degredados* continually increased, since sufficient manpower for the armed forces in India could be secured in no other way. Unlike the gypsies who were deported to Brazil and Angola, these *degredados*, whether officers or soldiers, did not take their womenfolk with them. This necessarily meant that a still smaller proportion of Portuguese women left Lisbon for Goa after 1630, and not, as Dr da Silva Correia claims, an astonishingly high number in the years 1630–70.

Of the women who did reach 'Golden Goa', the majority stayed there, or else they moved to the 'Province of the North', as the Portuguese called the fertile coastal region between Chaul (south of Bombay) and Damão, which they held until it was wrested from

[1] On the other hand, Dr da Silva Correia does certainly show that many of the Orphans of the Crown were remarkably fecund, as were some of their descendants, thus casting doubts on the assertions of several contemporaries, including Fernão de Queiroz S.J., that these women almost invariably either proved barren or else aborted in childbirth. Nevertheless, the fact remains that successive viceroys constantly complained to the Crown about the great lack of white men in Portuguese Asia and the paucity of their descendants. By 1871, there were only 2,500 of these *Descendentes* and in 1956 this number had shrunk to a little over 1,000 in a population totalling about half a million. Cf. C. R. Boxer, *Race Relations in the Portuguese Colonial Empire, 1415–1825* (Oxford, 1963), pp. 78–80, and the sources there quoted. Further research into this topic is clearly required starting with a rigorous analysis of the evidence adduced by Dr da Silva Correia.

them by the Marathas in 1739. While accurate statistics are lacking, all references to the presence of white women in other parts of Portuguese Asia indicate that they were very few and far between, even in places like Ceylon. For example, there was only one at Muscat in 1553, and only one at Macao in 1636. At Ternate and Tidore in the Spice Islands, the wives of the few Portuguese settlers (*moradores*) were all local women, according to sixteenth-century Spanish accounts; and the same was true of Amboina when the Dutch captured that island in 1605. There were a few white women in Zambesia, for reasons we shall shortly see; but on Moçambique island in 1822, after over three centuries of continuous Portuguese occupation, there were only six white families of European origin.[1]

One reason for this paucity of white women and their descendants was the fact that so many Portuguese men, including the *soldados* (as the unmarried men were called for centuries owing to their liability to military service) preferred to live with a harem of slave girls rather than to marry, at any rate in their younger and more virile days.[2] The Jesuit missionaries in particular, who had higher standards in this as in other respects than most of the Religious Orders in the East, never ceased to deplore the Portuguese proclivity for concubinage from the days of St Francis Xavier onwards. Their criticisms are amply confirmed from other sources which prove, as Padre Francisco de Sousa S.J. wrote in 1698, that a Portuguese in India who had hardly enough bread to eat insisted on maintaining a large household of slave-girls. These were often of the most varied origins, including Indians, Indonesians, Chinese, Japanese, Malays, Siamese and Africans.[3]

The orphan girls of the Crown, on reaching Goa, were originally

[1] Virginia Rau, 'Aspectos étnico-culturais da ilha de Moçambique em 1822', *Studia*, vol. XI (1963), pp. 134–5.

[2] Nautch-girls were also very popular with Portuguese males of all classes (although only wealthy *fidalgos* could afford to patronise the best), as Viceroys and Archbishops continually complained. C. R. Boxer, 'Fidalgos Portugueses e Bailadeiras Indianas. Séculos 17 e 18', 22-page reprint from the *Revista de História* of São Paulo, num. 56 (São Paulo, 1961), pp. 83–105.

[3] Francisco de Sousa, S. J., *Oriente Conquistado* (2 vols., Lisboa, 1710), vol. I. p. 740; C. R. Boxer, *Race Relations* (1963), pp. 59–65, and the sources there quoted. For an early example of such a mixed (and virtually polygamous) household, see the last will and testament of António de Faria de Sousa, d. Goa, 2 June 1548, in *Anais da Academia Portuguesa da Historia*, 2ª Série, vol. 20 (1971), pp. 163–8.

boarded out with respectable families until they could be married to a suitable man, which was apt to depend on the size and nature of the individual girl's dowry. In 1598, however, there was founded the *Recolhimento da Nossa Senhora da Serra* (Retirement House of Our Lady of the Mountain), largely through the efforts of the Augustinian Archbishop, Don Aleixo de Meneses. Girls admitted had to be white, Roman Catholic, and well-born. They included both the *orphãas del Rei* from Portugal as well as locally-born girls of similar status. Respectable widows, and wives abandoned by their husbands, or who were left there by them during a temporary absence from Goa, were also admitted as paying lodgers. This *Recolhimento* was run by the Santa Casa da Misericórdia, although the Crown provided for the upkeep of the orphans which it sent out annually, limited to twenty by the year 1617. Intended exclusively for honest and well-born girls, there were soon complaints that viceroys and governors were bringing pressure on the Board of Guardians of the Misericórdia to admit women of doubtful virtue, and the Crown promulgated a strictly-worded decree forbidding this practice in 1615.[1]

In order to avoid such an embarrassing mixture, the indefatigable Archbishop Meneses had founded another Retirement House, called that of Mary Magdalene, in 1610–11. This was intended to shelter women who had 'repented and been converted from their evil way of life', termed *arrependidas* or *convertidas*. Only white women were supposed to be admitted, but in point of fact Eurasians were in the majority from the start. This *Recolhimento* was likewise administered, financed and operated by the Misericórdia. Originally established in a large building next to the Jesuit College of St. Paul, it was moved in 1705 to a house built next to the Retirement House of the Mountain, where it remained until 1836.[2]

The term 'orphan' in Portuguese law covered not only a child who had lost both parents, but also only one, more particularly the father. The locally-born orphans who were admitted to Our Lady of the Mountain were supposed to be the children of fathers

---

[1] The history of this Retirement House is recorded in some detail both by José Frederico Ferreira Martins, *História da Misericórdia de Goa* (3 vols., Nova Goa, 1910–14), vol. II, pp. 201–86, and by Dr Germano da Silva Correia, *História da Colonização, passim*, but we badly need a new study which will pull their diffuse and rambling (but well-documented) accounts together.

[2] Same sources as in the previous note, with same comment.

who had died fighting the Muslim, heretic, or other enemies of the State of India. They were also supposed to be, by the regulations as revised in 1734, between the ages of 14 and 30, and 'good looking' into the bargain. At this period, the dowries granted to the inmates of Our Lady of the Mountain were given on a sliding-scale of preferences. First, 'to the daughters of the House'. Secondly, 'to the most virtuous, good-looking, and abandoned orphans'. Thirdly, to the daughters of 'people on the visiting-list' (i.e. persons in receipt of charity); and lastly to 'Orphans of the City', meaning presumably citizens of Goa in preference to those of other settlements in Portuguese Asia, such as Damão and Macao. There was also a ban (renewed in 1729) on the admission of bastard children and those 'of inferior quality'; although in point of fact bastard girls were often admitted both before and after this ruling. Specifically, the Board of Guardians resolved to admit (on 12 December 1729) a petitioner, Maria da Camara Coutinho, because she was the 'granddaughter of two viceroys of this State', on condition that this would not serve as a precedent for the admission of other bastard children who had not got the same exalted origin. On 1 March 1787, the Board of Guardians also voted to admit a girl whom everyone knew was the illegitimate daughter of the Governor-General, Guilherme de Sousa, but who was then described as his *afilhada* (god-daughter), a decision made easier by the fact that the Governor-General had offered to pay for her dowry and maintenance.[1]

Although the inmates of the Lady of the Mountain and of Mary Magdalene were supposed to be kept strictly separate, individuals were sometimes transferred from one institution to the other, despite the protests of the Board of Guardians, and despite the fact that this transfer was (in the eighteenth century) permitted for respectable married women from the former to the latter in certain circumstances, but never *vice versa*.

Both institutions strictly prohibited the admission of girls with 'New-Christian' (i.e. ancestral Jewish) blood, and both received legacies from pious testators which gave additional financial support to what they received from the Crown and from the Misericórdia. As noted above, the rules and regulations originally provided for the admission of legitimately born white girls only, but this was disregarded in practice almost from the start. A royal decree of

---

[1] Germano da Silva Correia, *História da Colonização*, vol. IV, pp. 50-1; J. F. Ferreira Martins, *História da Misericórdia de Goa*, vol. II, pp. 204 *et seq.*

24 January 1686, addressed to the Board of Guardians of the Misericórdia, rebuked them for admitting to the Recolhimento da Serra girls who were born of Hindu, Muslim, and Black African mothers; but there is no reason to suppose that this reprimand had any practical effect, since by this time the vast majority of children born in Portuguese Asia were Eurasians of one kind or another.[1]

In addition to these two Retirement Houses at Goa, there was also an Augustinian convent or Nunnery of Santa Monica, founded in the early seventeenth century after much foot-dragging and opposition locally, as well as reluctance on the part of the Crown. Archbishop Meneses, who had vainly tried to found one earlier, quoted the precedent of Spanish-America, where, so he said, there were fifteen convents in Mexico City alone, 'thirteen of professed nuns, and two of Retirement damsels'. The history of this Convent of Santa Monica has been discussed elsewhere, and it is sufficient to recall here that it became a kind of status symbol, into which the best families of Goa tried to get one or more of their daughters accepted as novices. Naturally, they had to provide a *dote* or dowry; and in the seventeenth century, the convent acquired the reputation of being very wealthy and more attractive to eligible heiresses than was marriage to some (usually impecunious and syphilitic) male.[2]

The question of dowries for the 'Orphans of the Crown', whether these were European or Asian born, provoked much official correspondence and legislation, some of it contradictory. A royal decree of the 24 November 1583 laid down that Viceroys could give minor government posts such as trading-agencies and below (*feitorias para baixo*) as dowries to the Orphans of the Crown on their marriage, provided the husband was suitably qualified, without obtaining royal confirmation. More substantial grants, such as captaincies of fortresses, could only be given pending

---

[1] '... que não fazieis nenhuma escolha nas orfãas que recebieis e sucedia muitas vezes serem ellas havidas por seus Pays de mulheres gentias, mouras, e cafras, e que dotandosse estas se deixasse de acudir as que lhe fazião conhecida ventagem, assy na diferença com que nascerão, como nos serviços que herdarão ...' (*alvará* of 24 Jan. 1686, *apud* Ferreira Martins, op. cit., II, p. 254).

[2] Fr. Agostinho de Santa Maria, O.E.S.A., *Historia da Fundação do Real Convento de Santa Monica da Cidade de Goa, Corte do Estado da India, e do Imperio Lusitano do Oriente* (Lisboa, 1699). Cf. also C. R. Boxer, *Portuguese Society in the Tropics, 1510–1800* (1965), pp. 28–39, and the sources there quoted.

royal confirmation. Writing to the Crown in February 1619, the Viceroy Count of Redondo complained that he had experienced great difficulty in marrying off the three orphans who had come out with him in his flagship, 'since so few men wish to marry with these orphans, as they are already old, and the men here are more interested in the value of the dowries than in the qualities of their potential brides'. This anticipates a seventeenth-century English writer's comparison of the virtue of toleration with 'a beautiful but poor gentlewoman, whom all will commend but none will marry'. In order to overcome the hesitations of prospective suitors, the Viceroy added a cash grant of 1,000 *xerafines* from the royal exchequer to supplement each of the minor government posts given as dowries. These posts were usually awarded on a triennial basis, and often had a long list of prior grantees when any vacancy occurred. The Viceroy concluded by stating that the Crown should consider some other way of attracting potential suitors for its orphans, 'because those of them who marry here do so both late and ill, and this has been the way in which most of those sent out have married hitherto'.[1]

Despite the Count of Redondo's allegations, some of these orphans did not do too badly; and when they were widowed, the grants were sometimes renewed; or else the widows received fresh grants in money, in land, or in minor government posts, to enable them to marry again. One of the three about whom the Count was so concerned in 1619, Dona Cherubina (Querumbina) de Sampaio, whom he married with a veteran soldier, Sebastian Veloso, was subsequently twice widowed and each time received a Crown dowry to help her to remarry, which she promptly did.[2] At an earlier date, Dona Francisca Peixoto, an orphan who had come out to India in 1563 and married there, had lost her husband in the great siege of Goa (1570–1), leaving her a widow with three small girls and two boys. She received a renewal of her original grant 'of the said office of judge of the Customs-House at Diu, for the said time of three years, for the person with whom she may marry, provided he is properly qualified for this post. This grant is made on the condition that she and her future husband allocate

---

[1] Viceroy Count of Redondo to the Crown, Goa, 20 February, 1619, in *Documentos Remettidos da India ou Livros das Monções* (5 vols., Lisboa, 1880–1935), vol. V, pp. 217–19.

[2] Germano da Silva Correia, *História da Colonização*, vol. IV, pp. 70–3.

from the income of the said office, the sum of one thousand *pardaus* to each of her daughters by her first husband, António Peixoto, in order to help them to get married . . .' This pattern, with suitable variations, was quite a common one.[1]

If some orphans married reasonably quickly and relatively well, and sometimes often, there were undoubtedly many instances of long delays and resultant hardships, such as the case of Victoria Mesquita, an orphan of the Crown who had come out to Goa in 1580 and married there in the same year. Her dowry was a minor post at Diu, but when her husband tried to claim it, he was excluded by a legal decision of the local High Court on the grounds that the royal confirmation was required. The City of Goa took up this case and forwarded all the necessary papers to the Crown at Lisbon in 1594, but ten years later no reply had been received. By this time the couple had four girls of marriageable age, and the City wrote to the Crown again asking for a favourable decision to be expedited, since otherwise the husband would be too old to fill the post, 'as he is already very aged'.[2]

Writing to the Crown in 1627, the Viceroy Count of Vidigueira repeated the Count of Redondo's complaint in almost the same terms: 'Sire, it is very difficult nowadays to find husbands for these orphans here, because the men are much more desirous of dowries in money than in posts . . . I therefore request Your Majesty for authority to supplement the post with a cash grant,' just as his predecessor had done in 1619.[3] This system of granting the twenty orphans of the Crown in the Recolhimento da Serra a dowry of a government post supplemented by a grant of 1,000 *xerafines* in cash was reconfirmed by a royal decree of 1647.[4] Thirty-two years later, the Governor General, António Paes de Sande, reported that owing to the increasing poverty of the royal exchequer in India, the cash grant of 1,000 *xerafines* was often replaced by the grant of a second government post, of less value that the first. He stated that at this period there were usually about 200 orphan girls in the Serra (including the twenty financed entirely by the Crown), and over sixty in the Mary Magdalene, since there was not room for all of them in the Serra. Both institutions were now being financed and

[1] Ibid., vol. II, pp. 188–9.
[2] Ibid., vol. II, pp. 298–9.
[3] Ibid., vol. II, p. 300.
[4] Ibid., vol. IV, p. 508.

maintained by a mixture of grants from the Crown and from the Misericórdia; but Paes de Sande asked the Crown to increase its contribution, since the Misericórdia was now very poor and had fallen on hard times.[1]

When the system of the 'Orphans of the King' had first been instituted in 1543–5, this had been done with the avowed intention of sending marriageable white girls to India and so increasing the white population. No provision was made for the orphaned Eurasian daughters of the Portuguese in India, who were much more numerous, and this omission inevitably provoked a stream of protests from the Municipal Council and the Misericórdia at Goa, in 1562, 1573, 1586, to mention only a few instances. They suggested that since there were already many respectable orphans at Goa, daughters of Portuguese men who had been killed fighting the enemies of the Cross and the Crown, there was no need to send out orphaned girls from Portugal to compete in the marriage-market with those who were locally born. Acknowledging these protests in 1587, the King replied: 'Although there are strong arguments on both sides in this matter … Yet I urge you to receive and look after those who are sent out from here,' as well as taking care of the local girls.[2] In the upshot, the system continued, with short intermittent breaks, for over another century, although, as we have seen, on a very reduced scale in the dispatch of white girls to the East after about 1630. I have the impression that by the mid-eighteenth century the dispatch of white girls from Lisbon had stopped, and that all the inmates were local girls.

With the economic decay of Portuguese Asia, resulting from the lengthy Dutch War (1600–63), and the loss of so many Portuguese possessions to the heretic Hollanders and the Muslim Arabs of Oman, the government posts available as dowries for orphans, whether of European origins or locally-born, decreased both in number and in value. By the mid-seventeenth century the Crown had, rather reluctantly, conceded that locally-born orphans should be treated on the same footing as those sent from Lisbon, once they were admitted to the Serra. Originally, it was stipulated that these local orphans must be girls whose fathers had been killed in battle; but in 1664 the Crown waived even this restriction, although

[1] Ibid., vol. IV, pp. 677–81.
[2] Ibid., vol. II, pp. 324–6.

stating that preference should be given to these when candidates applied for admission.[1]

As regards the dowries, the most valuable and sought-after of these were no longer government posts, or even the captaincies of fortresses, but the grant of a village, or villages, in the 'Province of the North', the Portuguese-controlled territory between Chaul and Damão, which extended inland for a distance averaging about thirty miles. This region had come under Portuguese control by the second half of the sixteenth century and was administered from Bassein (Baçaim), a walled city whose inhabitants prided themselves on being the most aristocratic in Portuguese India, hence its sobriquet 'Dom Baçaim'. These villages (*aldeias*) were usually quite small in extent, only a few acres of palm-groves and/or rice-fields with the village where the cultivators lived. But they produced a relatively high income from the rich soil and the careful husbandry with which they were worked by a very docile and cheap labour-force, whether these villagers were christianised or still Hindu.[2]

These *aldeias* were granted by the Crown (or by the Viceroy in the name of the Crown) for one, two or three lives; but they often tended to become hereditary in return for the payment of an annual *foro* or quit-rent to the Crown. The grantee might be either a man or a woman, but there was a general tendency to grant them as a dowry to deserving widows and orphans. In 1561, for example, the widow of a gunner (*bombardeiro*) who had received the grant of such an *aldeia*, had her grant renewed for three lives, 'on condition that she should remarry with a gunner or with someone who would become a gunner'.[3] By the end of the sixteenth century, the usual practice was to grant these *aldeias* for three lives, with the obligation of (a) paying an annual *foro* or quit-rent to the Crown, (b) maintaining an Arab horse and a musket (*espingarda*) for local defence, (c) the grantee residing with his or her family in the *aldeia* concerned.[4] The system had obvious affinities with the *encomienda* in contemporary Spanish America, and probably derived from similar

[1] Ibid., vol. IV, pp. 46–8.

[2] We do not have an adequate study of the *aldeias do Norte* in the sixteenth to eighteenth centuries, but whoever decides to tackle this promising topic will find much of interest in Raquel Soeiro de Brito, *Goa e as Praças do Norte* (Lisboa, 1960).

[3] Germano da Silva Correia, *História da Colonização*, vol. II, p. 167. In this particular instance, the obligation to marry a gunner was later dispensed with.

[4] Ibid., vol. II, pp. 353–5.

medieval Iberian origins of the Reconquest period. From descriptions of the life led by the owners of these *aldeias*, both male and female, by the Abbé Carré, Gemelli-Careri, and other travellers in the second half of the seventeenth century, we can see that they often lived high, wide, and handsomely, at a time when the rest of Portuguese India, including once-Golden Goa, was plunged in poverty.[1]

When these *aldeias* were granted in the female line, as was often, though not invariably the case, the condition was sometimes made that the orphan or the widow involved should 'marry a Portuguese born in the kingdom of Portugal'. In 1628, for example, an orphan of the Crown, Dona Juliana de Gois, who had reached Goa four years earlier but who was still unmarried, received the grant of an *aldeia do Norte* on this condition.[2] The same clause, incidentally, was sometimes applied in the grants of captaincies of fortresses which were given as dowries to orphans, such as the captaincy of Asserim in 1626, and the captaincy of Chaul in 1627.

In December 1681, the municipal council of Damão protested to the Crown against this clause compelling the female grantees of *aldeias* to marry European-born Portuguese to the exclusion of Asian-born (most of whom, by this time, were Eurasians). They complained that this was unfair to any sons of the marriage, who were automatically excluded from inheriting their mother's *aldeias* by this clause, which ensured its descent in the female line. In any event, these stipulations were not always rigorously enforced; but it is clear from many contemporary sources such as Diogo do Couto, Nicolao Manucci, François Dellon, the Abbé Carré, and Gemelli-Careri, that the parents (and especially the mothers) of Eurasian heiresses to rich *aldeias* were desperately anxious to marry their daughters to European-born Portuguese, or better still (if the Abbé Carré is to be credited) to French or other Roman Catholic Europeans.[3]

---

[1] *The Travels of the Abbé Carré, 1672-1674* (Hakluyt Society edition by C. Fawcett and R. Burn, 3 vols., London, 1947), vol. I, pp. 191-4, and vol. III, pp. 724-67; Surendranath Sen (ed.), *The Indian Travels of Thevenot and Careri* (New Delhi, 1949), pp. 159-60, 179, 187.

[2] Germano da Silva Correia, *História da Colonização*, vol. III, p. 457.

[3] Sources quoted in note (27) above and in C. R. Boxer, *Race Relations in the Portuguese Colonial Empire, 1415-1825* (1963), p. 78; Germano da Silva Correia, *História da Colonização*, vol. IV, pp. 172-3, for the protest of the City Council of Damão in 1681.

The death-rate among Portuguese men in Asia, due to a combination of continual warfare, sexual over-indulgence, and tropical diseases, meant that their widows were often left as heads of households with authority to administer the children's share of the estate until the latter came of age. This provoked the Municipal Council of Goa to write to the Crown in 1605, complaining that orphans frequently did not receive their due, since the widow, as head of the family (*cabeça do casal*) retained the children's share of the inheritance without consenting to an immediate distribution of the estate as between herself and the children, which, under Portuguese as under Castilian law, was her legal obligation.[1] Moreover, such a widow would often remarry, and the stepfather would then manage and perhaps dissipate the children's share. Either way, when the children eventually claimed their inheritance, it had either disappeared altogether or had been greatly reduced. The council pointed out that in Portugal, where most of the gentry lived on their income from landed property, there was not much chance of a widow either alienating or dissipating it. But in India [Asia], where men did not usually live on their income from land, but on the profits of their monetary investments in the interport trade of Asia, widows should not be allowed to administer their children's share of the deceased's estate nor to function as *cabeça do casal*. The Crown agreed in principle, and decreed in 1607 that on a man's death, the division of the estate, as between the widow and the children, should be made forthwith, and the children's share should be deposited with some trustworthy executor (*curador*) who should invest it without risking it ('*que possa trazer a ganho sem o arriscar*'); rather a tall order, incidentally, at a time when the seaborne trade of Portuguese Asia was experiencing such heavy losses at the hands of its European and Asian enemies.[2]

The Crown did, however, authorise the Viceroy to make exceptions, allowing competent and intelligent widows to function as *cabeça do casal* and to administer their children's patrimony until they came of age. This was quite often done, especially in the administration of the landed estates of the *aldeias do Norte*, which, as we have seen, became increasingly important as a source of income when the seaborne trade of Portuguese Asia declined. There was also a number of instances in which widows were allowed to

---

[1] *Documentos Remettidos da India on Livros das Monções*, vol. I, p. 110.
[2] Germano da Silva Correia, *História da Colonização*, vol. III, pp. 315–21.

administer and operate the shipping belonging to their deceased husband, on their own behalf and on behalf of their children. Among them was Dona Luisa da Silveira, widow of Dom Francisco de Sousa, former Governor of Hormuz, who was authorised in August 1622 'to function as head of the family, ordering to sail for Goa the ships of her late husband which were still at sea, including a carrack (*nau grande*), a pinnace, and a galliot in Sindh, a ship fitted out in Chaul, and a galliot bound for this city which put into Dabul with eight [Arabian] horses on board'. It would be interesting to have more information about these widows who functioned as *cabeça do casal*, whether in the *aldeias do Norte* or as shipowners and operators.[1]

I mentioned in the last chapter that the Castilian Crown experienced some trouble with the *Oidores* or High Court Judges of Spanish-America, who tended to marry Creole heiresses in the area of their jurisdiction despite reiterated royal prohibition of this practice. Exactly the same thing occurred in Portuguese India, where the *Ouvidores* and senior magistrates tended to marry Eurasian heiresses with property in the villages of the North, although this was likewise repeatedly prohibited on paper. Among them was Dr Luis Mergulhão Borges, a Judge of the High Court (*Relação*) who married a wealthy widow who had outlived two previous husbands in 1629. Some seventy-five years later, the Viceroy informed the Crown: 'Judges usually marry in Goa with the heiresses of the villages of the North.' There is every reason to suppose that they continued to do so until the loss of the Province of the North to the Marathas in 1739.[2]

As we shall see in the next chapter, and as readers of foreign travellers' accounts of Portuguese Asia are well aware, the Eurasian ladies and women of Golden Goa have usually had 'a bad press', being accused of excessive pride, slothfulness, and immorality. To a large extent, these allegations are borne out by the official correspondence of the Viceroys, archbishops, and Inquisitors of Goa with the Crown. Nor could anything else be expected in a male-dominated society where the seclusion of women was carried to extremes, and where children were brought up in households where

[1] Ibid., vol. III, pp. 354, 357, 358–9, 381.
[2] Ibid., vol. II, pp. 405–17; Ibid., vol. IV, p. 243 ('Os desembargadores ordinariamente casavam em Goa com as herdeiras das aldeias do Norte . . .'); Ibid., vol. V. p. 374.

they often had far more to do with female slaves than with their own parents. But there were also some women brought up in these compromising and demoralising surroundings who by sheer force of character remained uncontaminated, and who acquitted themselves admirably in times of stress and danger.

The heroic defenders of Diu in both the epic sieges of 1538 and 1545, included a number of women, both European and Asian-born, who distinguished themselves alike in nursing the wounded and in fighting alongside the men. The most celebrated was the elderly Isabel Fernandes, *a velha de Diu*, 'the old woman of Diu', as she was subsequently called. Writing to the Queen-Regent of Portugal in 1559, to remind the Crown that she had not yet received any adequate reward for her services, she stated that of eighteen sons who were born to her only one remained alive, all the others having been killed in the service of the Crown.[1] The women of Chaul and of Goa also came to the help of the Crown in these crises, freely offering their personal jewelry and ornaments to the perennially impecunious royal Exchequer.

A wealthy widowed lady of Cochin, Dona Luisa da Silva, with an enormous slave-household, was famous for the charity with which she relieved the passengers and crews of outward-bound Indiamen when they arrived at that port suffering from scurvy and malnutrition.[2] Another wealthy widow nearly a century later acted in the same way at the great siege of Mombasa (1696–8).[3] When homeward-bound Indiamen were wrecked off the coast of Natal and the survivors had to trek overland to Lourenço Marques, Inhambane, or Sofala, the women sometimes withstood the hardships better than did the men.[4] Most famous of these ladies was the beautiful and courageous Dona Leonor de Sá, who vainly strove to encourage her pusillanimous husband and who died of shame when

---

[1] Ibid., vol. II, pp. 508–26.

[2] Fernão de Queiroz, S.J., *Conquista Espiritual e Temporal da Ilha de Ceilão, 1687* (ed. Colombo, 1916), p. 433; Germano da Silva Correia, *História da Colonização*, vol. IV, p. 433, and vol. V, pp. 43–4. She told the Jesuits in December 1635: 'Bring as many as you like, Reverend Fathers, for thanks be to God there is room and service for everyone', and she was not satisfied until she had accommodated over 300 on this occasion.

[3] C. R. Boxer and Carlos de Azevedo, *Fort Jesus and the Portuguese in Mombasa, 1593–1729* (London, 1959), p. 55.

[4] C. R. Boxer (ed. and trans.), *The Tragic History of the Sea, 1589–1622* (Cambridge, 1959), pp. 103–4.

she and her children were stripped naked (but not otherwise harmed) by 'the Kaffirs'.[1] There was also an equivalent of the celebrated Basque male impersonator, Catalina de Erauso, alias *La Monja Alferez* (1595–1650), in Portuguese India, though she was a Brazilian by birth. Dona Maria Ursula de Abreu e Lencastre was born at Rio de Janeiro, and in order to escape marriage to a man she disliked, she enlisted under the name of Baltasar de Couto Cardoso as a marine in a warship bound for Lisbon. She sailed for India in the last year of the seventeenth century, and distinguished herself in several battles during the following fourteen years without her true sex being discovered. She finally rescued her captain, Afonso Teixeira Arrais de Melo e Mendonça, when the latter was in imminent danger of being killed or captured by the enemy; but she was seriously wounded when doing so, and her sex was revealed. Fittingly enough, the captain married her when she recovered, and they had a child named João. In recognition of her services as a soldier, she was given a grant of two palm-groves at Chaul in the Province of the North, on which, we may hope, she and her husband lived happily ever after.[2]

The ladies of these miniscule if profitable 'villages of the North' make an interesting contrast with those who ruled the often huge *prazos* or landed estates of Zambesia. The *prazos* were originally lands which Portuguese adventurers in this region had secured from Bantu chiefs, either by agreement or by conquest, and which were inhabited by a free African population (*colonos*) together with the African slaves of the Portuguese owner. The *prazeros* originally paid a *foro* or quit-rent to some ruling Bantu overlord, which was later transferred to the Crown. The position they had attained by 1667 was thus described by a Jesuit missionary, Manuel Barreto, who knew the region well:

'The Portuguese lords of these lands have in their hands that same power and jurisdiction as had the Kaffir chiefs [*Fumos*] from whom they were taken, because the terms of quit-rent [*foro*] were made on that condition. For this reason, they are like German potentates, since they can lay down the law in everything, put people to death, declare war, and levy taxes. Perhaps they

[1] James Duffy, *Shipwreck and Empire* (Harvard University Press, 1959), pp. 45–6.
[2] Germano da Silva Correia, *História da Colonização*, vol. v, pp. 565–74.

sometimes commit great barbarities in all this; but they would not be respected as they should be by their vassals if they did not enjoy the same power as the chiefs whom they succeeded.'[1]

The more powerful *prazeros* maintained private armies composed of the free Negroes who lived on their lands, with a hard core of their own more disciplined warrior slaves (*achikunda*). These armies might amount to between 5,000 and 25,000 men when they took the field, although they were apt to dissolve as easily as they were formed if anything went wrong. The *prazeros* frequently feuded with each other, aside from being engaged in perennial warfare with unsub- dued and hostile tribes. For these and other reasons, the *prazos* changed in ownership and in extent very rapidly, and the *prazeros* themselves tended to become completely Africanised within two or three generations, living as they did with many African free and slave concubines, and sometimes marrying with the daughters of Bantu chiefs. With the object of averting this development, and in order to bring these lands under the effective control of the Crown, some of the *prazos* were transformed into entailed estates which were granted by the Crown for three successive lives on payment of an annual quit-rent in gold dust. Theoretically, these Crown-*prazos* (*prazos da Coroa*) were granted to white women born of Portuguese parents, who could only secure or retain the *prazo* on condition that they married with a white Portuguese man. Male children of these unions were excluded from the succession, the *prazos da Coroa* descending only in the female line, with the same proviso that the heiress must marry a white man, as had been enacted for some of the Indian *Aldeias do Norte* at an earlier period (p. 76 above). A Crown-*prazo* granted to a family on these conditions was originally for three lives only, after which it was supposed to revert to the Crown. Failure to cultivate the land properly, the marriage of the lady owner with a coloured man, or her failure to reside upon the estate, likewise carried the penalty of the *prazo* reverting to the Crown. Some legislative endeavours were also made to limit the size of the *prazos*.

These conditions were soon and increasingly disregarded. Some *prazos* swelled to enormous proportions, rivalling those of the largest *fazendas* in the backlands of colonial Brazil. The obligation to

[1] C. R. Boxer, *The Portuguese Seaborne Empire, 1415–1825* (London, 1969), pp. 139–42, for the above and what follows.

6

cultivate the land properly was generally ignored, as there was no market for an exportable agricultural surplus. The *prazeros* therefore contented themselves with growing enough crops to feed their household and slaves. White men were so few in the Zambesi valley, and their expectation of life was so short, that the *prazo* heiresses, the *Donas de Zambesia* ('Ladies of Zambesia'), in the eighteenth-century, often married with the better acclimatised Mulattoes, or with Indo-Portuguese, or with Indian traders from Goa, many of whom also became *prazo*-holders in the late eighteenth and early nineteenth centuries. Allen Isaacman has recently documented the increasing Africanisation of this peculiar Portuguese (or Afro-Indo-Portuguese) society, and the futile efforts made by the Crown to check this development, which accelerated from *c.* 1750 onwards.[1] The principal *prazo* families also intermarried with each other, although considerable inter-family feuding likewise persisted. As elsewhere in the tropical and sub-tropical worlds (pp. 19, 25, above), the women proved more resistant to disease and more long-lived than the men. Several of the *Donas de Zambesia* took two, three, or four successive spouses, and some of them continued their marital escapades until they were eighty years old.

Increasingly frequent inter-marriage with coloured men did not mean that the *Donas de Zambesia* would not marry a suitable white man if they had the chance. In the short period between 1750 and 1775, for example, three governors of the *Rios de Sena* ('Rivers of Sena', the Portuguese term for Zambesia) married into *prazo* families, bringing with them positions and titles which the older families eagerly sought. But, as Isaacman shows, the dearth of unattached white males forced the *Donas de Zambesia* to seek unions with men who were well below them in social standing, and increasingly dark-skinned in colour. They included the Goan traders of pure Indian blood, who began to reside in Zambesia after the abolition of restrictions on their residence in the middle of the eighteenth-century. By 1789, the Goans had achieved a dominant social and economic position in *prazero* society. Their descendants retained this position throughout the nineteenth century, and they were joined by a small number of lower-class Portuguese *degredados*, who were able to marry into some of the traditional families on account of their white blood. But given the total absence of white

[1] Allen F. Isaacman, *Mozambique. The Africanization of a European Institution, The Zambesi prazos, 1750–1902* (University of Wisconsin Press, 1972).

women in Zambesia, the *Donas* and their descendants continued to darken with each generation. As Isaacman writes: 'The infusion of Portuguese blood was, therefore, marginal, and successive generations were absorbed into the growing mestizo community. They became the characteristic racial group in the Zambesi, and were collectively known by the African term *muzungu*.'[1]

Despite the definitive nature of Isaacman's book, it is clear that some of the *Donas de Zambesia* would repay further research in their own right, as interesting and forceful personalities who left their mark on the society of their times. There was one, Dona Catarina, who vainly tried to bribe the young Viceroy of India, Dom Luís de Menezes, Count of Ericeira, with a gold service 'of greater weight than artistry', in order to secure a post for her husband.[2] There was Dona Ignez Pessoa de Almeida Castello-Branco, who in the mid-eighteenth century reigned over the huge *prazos* of Cheringoma and Gorongoza, and who controlled some 6,000 *achikunda* or slave-warriors.[3] Most famous (or infamous, perhaps), was Dona Ignez Correia Cardozo, the powerful owner of the *prazo* of Luabo among others, in the mid-eighteenth century. Married to an ex-Governor of Macao, António José Telles de Menezes, she threw him out of her house after six months, wishing to kill or divorce him in order to marry her latest lover, a Portuguese high official (?David Marques Pereira, the General of the Rivers?). Not content with driving him away, she killed with her armed slaves anyone who dared to give the unfortunate man any shelter or hospitality, including some women and children, and a Portuguese army officer who had been sent to reinstate him. While engaged in this campaign, the sanguinary Amazon assured the garrison commander of Sena that he had nothing to fear from her, since she was not engaged in any rebellion against the Crown, but was resolved to kill Telles de Menezes wherever or whenever she might find him. She never actually caught up with him; but she did chase him out of East

---

[1] Allen F. Isaacman, *Mozambique* (1972), pp. 58–9.

[2] Dom Jozé Barbosa, *Epitome da Vida do . . . Senhor D. Luiz Carlos de Menezes . . . quinto Conde da Ericeira* (Lisboa, 1743), p. 117. The same anecdote is repeated in Sebastião José de Carvalho, *Elogio de D. Luiz Carlos de Menezes, quinto Conde da Ericeira* (Lisboa, 1757), p. 17, where, however, the 'peças de ouro de mayor pezo que feitio' have been up-graded into 'huma baixella de ouro, tão custosa pelo grande pezo do ouro, como pelo primor do feitio'. Neither account gives Dona Catarina's surname.

[3] Allen F. Isaacman, *Mozambique* (1972), p. 190.

Africa, and he next appears as Governor of Timor, with the width of the Indian Ocean between himself and his estranged wife.[1]

The *Donas de Zambesia* were, I presume, something unique in the Portuguese colonial world or, for that matter, in any other. They were certainly very different from the women of Macao, who led far more cribbed, cabined and confined lives in the grandiloquently named but narrowly bounded City of the Name of God in China. Founded in or around the years 1555–7, there were, in all probability, no white women among the original settlers (*moradores*). These latter did not at first mix with the Chinese population of neighbouring Heungshan, and the women with whom they lived were Japanese, Malays, Indonesians and Indians, many of them being slaves.[2] Within a short time, however, a substantial population of Chinese settled in the growing port. This quickly became an *entrepôt* for the China-Japan trade, since the ruling Ming dynasty forbade its own subjects to trade with Japan, or the Japanese with China. The Portuguese men, therefore, soon started to intermarry with Chinese women and, still more often, to use them as concubines and indentured girl-servants, *mui-tsai*. These latter were frequently little more than slaves, in effect; although on the other hand, they were often adopted by childless couples, by widowers or by widows, and brought up as daughters and members of the household.

Padre Alonso Sánchez, a Spanish Jesuit from the Philippines, who paid two extended visits to Macao in 1583–5, noted that 'the Chinese women are naturally reserved, honest, humble, and very submissive to their husbands, hard-workers and house-proud ... The Portuguese of Macao marry with them more willingly than with any other women, because of the many virtues which adorn the former.' So enthusiastic was Padre Sánchez over these paragons, that in his scheme for the conquest of China by the Spaniards, supported by Portuguese, Japanese and Filipino auxiliary troops, which he laid before Philip II in 1588, he stressed the advantages

[1] C. R. Boxer, *Fidalgos in the Far East. Fact and Fancy in the History of Macao, 1550–1770* (The Hague, 1948), pp. 246–9, and the sources there quoted; Allen F. Isaacman, *Mozambique*, p. 105.

[2] C. R. Boxer (ed. and trans.), *South China in the Sixteenth Century, 1550–1575* (London, 1953), pp. xxxiii–xxxvii; Manuel Teixeira, *Os Macaenses* (Macau, 1965), pp. 7–26, and the sources there quoted.

which would result from the intermarriage of Iberian *conquistadores* with Chinese women. These latter, he claimed, were as intelligent and capable as were aristocratic Castilian ladies, in sharp contrast to the Amerindian and *mestiza* women of Spanish-America whom no respectable Spaniard wished to marry. The children born of Iberian fathers and Chinese mothers would, he asserted, be in every respect the equals of pure-bred Europeans. They could become governors, viceroys, bishops, and high officials, something which was both undesirable and impossible for the *mestizos* of Mexico and Peru.[1]

Philip 'the prudent' politely rejected Padre Sánchez's bellicose projects for the conquest of China; but the Portuguese of Macao continued to marry and to cohabit with Chinese and Eurasian women, if only because no others were available to them, since few or none of the 'Orphans of the Crown' ever seem to have got that far. Peter Mundy, the Cornish traveller who has left us one of the best accounts of the City of the Name of God in its prime, noted in 1637: 'By report but one woman in this town that was born in Portugal; their wives [being] either Chinesas or of that race heretofore married to Portugals.' He was much impressed by the beauty of some of the Eurasian children whom he saw in the house of António de Oliveira Aranha, erstwhile Captain-Major of the Japan Voyage, where he was hospitably entertained and lodged: 'There were at that time in the house three or four very pretty children, daughters to the said Senhor Antonio and his kindred, that except in England, I think not in the world to be overmatched for their pretty feature and complexion, their habit or dressing becoming them as well, adorned with precious jewels and costly apparel, their uppermost garment being little kimaones or Japanese coats (*kimono*) which graced them also.'[2]

Peter Mundy has also left us an interesting description with a pen-and-ink drawing of the peculiar dress worn by Macaonese women when they went outside their houses. It consisted essentially of two large pieces of silk, one used as a veil-cum-shawl, and the other as a petticoat. Although Peter Mundy and later foreign visitors to Macao, such as Gemelli Careri, vouched for the essential modesty

[1] *Apud* F. Colín, S.J.—Pablo Pastells, S.J., *Labor Evangelica de . . . la Compañía de Jesús en . . . Filipinas* (3 vols., Barcelona, 1904), Tomo I, pp. 438–45, and especially p. 443.

[2] C. R. Boxer, *Fidalgos in the Far East, 1550–1770* (1948), pp. 127–8.

of this traditional *saraça* (a term evidently of Malay origin), it was formally banned by Bishop Dom Alexandre Pedrosa Guimarães in a pastoral which he published on 1 April 1779. This ban aroused such violent opposition from the women and their menfolk, that it was apparently one of the reasons why that prelate left precipitately for Lisbon nine months later. However, the *saraça* was gradually replaced in the early nineteenth century by a black silk hooded cape termed the *dó*, which was probably of European (Azorean?) origin, and survived till within living memory.[1]

Although the dress of the Macaonese women was Asian rather than European for centuries, their religion ensured that culturally they would remain in the European rather than the Chinese orbit, despite the paucity of European women and the tenuousness of Macao's maritime connection with Portugal. Whereas the *Donas de Zambesia* became steadily more Africanised in the course of the eighteenth century, the upper-class ladies of Macao did not become more Sinified, although in the last quarter of the eighteenth century they were still speaking a local *patois* rather than correct Portuguese, and only a few of them wore European-style dress rather than the traditional *saraça*. As elsewhere in the Portuguese world, these upper-class women were noted for the seclusion and the retirement in which they lived, 'and when they go out, they do so inside their closed palanquins', as a visiting Portuguese naval officer noted in 1776, and as depicted in the contemporary Chinese chronicle of Macao. The above-mentioned naval officer, while acknowledging the secluded lives led by the ladies of Macao, added somewhat unfairly, 'they are usually proud and lazy, because their activities are limited to making children.'[2] In one instance at least, the process of procreation was preceded by a violent and stormy romance which divided the citizens into two rival camps, and is worth recalling briefly here.

Both protagonists were of exotically mixed blood. The man,

[1] G. F. Gemelli-Careri, *A Voyage round the World* (reprinted from A. and J. Churchill, *A Collection of Voyages and Travels*, vol. IV, pp. 1–606, London, 1744), p. 391; C. A. Montalto de Jesus, *Historic Macao* (Hong Kong, 1902), p. 41 *n*; Manuel Teixeira, *O Trajo Feminino em Macau do século XVI ao século XVIII* (Macao, 1969). Senhora Ana Maria Amaro is engaged in further research on this subject, particularly on the *dó*, which we may hope will be published soon.

[2] Report of N. Fernandes da Fonseca (Jan. 1776), *apud* J. Caetano Soares, *Macau e a Assistência* (1950), pp. 231–2.

António de Albuquerque Coelho, a captain of marines when he first came to Macao in 1706, had been born at Camutá in Brazil about 1682, the illegitimate son of a Portuguese *fidalgo* and a local woman with white, Amerindian and Negro blood in her veins, in about equal proportions. The girl, Maria de Moura, was only seven years old in 1706, and her very mixed ancestry included a Portuguese great-grandfather and a Japanese great-grandmother. She was of legitimate birth and lived in the house of her grandmother, Maria de Vasconcelos, after the death of her parents, the child being likewise the richest heiress in Macao. Presumably on this last account, António de Albuquerque attempted to become betrothed to the little girl, but her grandmother and other relatives flatly refused their consent, on the reasonable grounds that she was far too young. Albuquerque, however, secured the powerful support of the local Jesuits in pressing his suit, which he continued by correspondence when he returned to Goa, and renewed in person when he came again to Macao in 1708.[1]

On this occasion, if not before, Albuquerque got the cantankerous Bishop, Dom João do Casal, and his Vicar-General, the Canon Lourenço Gomes, on his side as well as the grandmother's own father-confessor. This combined ecclesiastical pressure proved too much for Maria de Vasconcelos, who, protesting bitterly, saw her grand-child abducted from her house and formally betrothed to Albuquerque in the church of St. Anthony on 30 June 1709. The actual marriage was not celebrated until 22 August 1710, when the bride was all of eleven years; and in the interval Albuquerque's rivals and enemies made several abortive attempts to assassinate him. In one of these, he received a wound which necessitated the amputation of his right arm above the elbow. Local tradition claims that when he sent to ask his betrothed if she was still prepared to marry him, she answered that she would do so even if he lost both legs. Early in 1712, the young mother gave birth to a girl, who survived only seven days, and in July 1714 to a boy, whose arrival was celebrated with city-wide rejoicings, cut short by Maria de Moura's premature death ten days later, at the age of fifteen.

The considerable mixture of Chinese blood which the Macaonese

---

[1] For this and what follows see my *Fidalgos in the Far East* (1948), pp. 199–221, corrected by the additional documentation published later by J. Caetano Soares, *Macau e a Assistência* (1950), pp. 54–72, and Manuel Teixeira, *Macau e a sua diocese*, VII, *Padres da Diocese de Macau*, 1967), pp. 372–5, 487–519.

absorbed in the course of centuries, derives largely from the co-habitation of Portuguese and Eurasian male householders with their *mui-tsai*. These latter were unwanted Chinese female children who were sold by their parents into domestic service for a fixed number of years (normally forty), or for the term of their natural lives. The practice of selling such girls to the inhabitants of Macao started very early, and it continued for over three centuries despite re-iterated prohibitions by both the Portuguese and the Chinese authorities. As mentioned previously, while some of these children were badly exploited and ill-treated, others were brought up as if they were the owners' own children and were often provided for in their last wills and testaments. The surviving records of the Santa Casa da Misericórdia bear evidence of this.[1] They recall the similar bequests made in favour of slaves and servants under similar circumstances on the other side of the Portuguese world in the Azores and at Bahia (pp. 33, 61 above).

As with these latter, such bequests were often made with the condition that the beneficiary should continue to serve some rela-tive or member of the family for a few years before collecting the inheritance or the dowry. Before the end of the Japan trade in 1639–40, it was a common practice for the testator to have the legacy invested, in whole or in part, in the Japan Voyage or the *carreira de Japão*, either in Chinese silks or in Japanese (or in Spanish-American) silver. Some bequests were made on condition that the recipient would marry a specified individual, or a person of a certain category, such as a Portuguese, or a Christian Chinese. Bequests to unconverted slaves or *mui-tsai* usually specified that they should become converts to Christianity before receiving the legacy. A few examples from the period 1590–1630 will show how closely the pattern at Macao conformed to that obtaining elsewhere in the Portuguese world.

Manuel Gomes bequeathed to 'a Chinese girl named Maria, whom I bought to bring up as my own daughter,' the sum of 150 silver taels' worth of silk. This was to be invested on her behalf by Senhora Juliana do Fazil, whom the testator implored to look after the little girl until she came of age and could marry a suitable

[1] Arquivo da Santa Casa da Misericórdia, Macao, Codice 15, whence all the following quotations are taken. It is an eighteenth-century copy dated 1 June 1750, and I am indebted to Senhor Luís Gonzaga Gomes for permission to consult this codex at Macao in March 1971, and for securing photos.

person, preferably 'a Portuguese, a good man'. Half of the 150 taels was to be invested in the Japan trade and the other half in the India trade.

A widow named Luisa Lobato freed a Japanese slave-girl named Magdalena, and bequeathed her the sum of ten *pardaos de reales*, 'on condition that she should be brought up in the house of my co-godparent (*compadre*) Fernão de Palhares, until she marries. And if she should misbehave and leave his house, she will not be given the ten *pardaos de reales*, which will be given instead to the Misericórdia.' A wealthy widow, Joanna Pestana, made several bequests, ranging in value from 100 to 10 *pardaos de reales*, as dowries for the daughters of various friends, all of which would revert to the Misericórdia if the legatees died before they were married. She also freed and endowed some of her slaves and *mui-tsai* in the same way, including 'a Chinese girl called Anna, to whom I give her freedom together with the sum of 20 *pardaos de reales* for her marriage. And should she die before being married, this money will go to the Misericórdia.'

With the help of these and other charitable bequests, the Misericórdia of Macao, like those elsewhere, arranged for a limited number of foundlings to be put out to paid foster-mothers until they were seven years old. It likewise endowed a few but respectable orphan girls of marriageable age, and operated a short-lived *Recolhimento* (Retirement House) for widows and orphans between 1727 and 1737.[1]

Although the Crown had only reluctantly sanctioned the establishment of the Augustinian Convent of Santa Monica at Goa, and had (in 1607) peremptorily ordered that no other Nunnery should be founded in Portuguese Asia, yet a Convent of the Poor Clares was founded at Macao by a group of Spanish Franciscan Sisters from Manila in 1633, without the royal consent having been obtained. The municipal council (or senate) of Macao protected and supported the institution since that date, providing an annual income derived from a surtax of 1% levied on all *fazendas grossas* imported into Macao.[2] By the original agreement of 1633, the number of nuns was limited to forty, and preference was always given to the daughters of the citizens who had served, or were actually serving, on the

---

[1] J. Caetano Soares, *Macau e a Assistência* (1950), pp. 350–3.

[2] *Fazendas grossas* included a wide variety of commodities, such as sandalwood, shark's fins, cotton, putchuck, coarse cloth, etc.

municipal council. In 1692, the Senators promised 'to pay this 1%
punctually, while the nuns on their side are obliged to receive every
five years one daughter of a citizen without a dowry'. The waspish
Spanish Dominican, Fr. Domingo Fernández Navarrete, who spent
some time at Macao in the years 1658–9 and 1669–70, reported not
without a touch of malicious humour: 'When the Tartars conquered
China, those nuns, fearing lest the invaders might also come over
into Macao, and some disaster might befall them, petitioned the
City to send them to some other place. Having weighed and considered the matter the Senators answered "that the Reverend
Sisters need not worry, for if anything threatened, they would
presently repair to their convent with a couple of barrels of gun-
powder, and blow them all up, which would deliver them from
any ill designs of the Tartars". An excellent method of comforting
the poor afflicted creatures!'[1]

Fortunately this danger did not materialise, but there were other
times when the Senators and the Poor Clares did not see eye to eye.
In 1746, for example, the Senate complained that the convent
attracted all the local rich girls with their dowries, thus spoiling the
marriage-market for expectant but impecunious bachelors. The
Senators also alleged that while the nuns were lending substantial
sums of money on *respondencia* (bottomry) to Armenian, Spanish,
and French traders, they refused to lend any money to the Senate,
on the plea of poverty. Both criticisms recall those made against
the nuns of Santa Monica at Goa and against those of the Desterro
at Bahia, respectively. But, as had happened at those two places,
amicable relations were soon re-established, since the convent was a
status symbol and the citizens needed it as a refuge for their unmarried daughters.[2]

[1] J. S. Cummins (ed.), *The Travels and Controversies of Friar Domingo
Navarrete, O.P., 1618–1688* (2 vols., Hakluyt Society, Cambridge, 1962),
vol. II, pp. 261–2. Navarrete is certainly open to criticism at times, as his
editor fully realises and makes perfectly clear. It is therefore absurd of E. J.
Burrus, S.J., to accuse J. S. Cummins of 'anti-Jesuit animus', as he does in
Kino Writes to the Duchess (Rome, 1965), p. 45 *n*, thus marring an otherwise
judicious and scholarly book.

[2] C. R. Boxer, *Portuguese Society in the Tropics, 1510–1800* (1965), pp. 36–9,
64–5, 92–4; J. Russell-Wood, *Fidalgos and Philanthropists, 1550–1755* (London,
1968), pp. 58, 113, 134, 177–9, 312, 321–2. As mentioned previously, Susan
Soeiro is now engaged on a doctoral dissertation on the Poor Clares' Convent
of the Desterro at Bahia, which will undoubtedly add much to our knowledge of
its social history.

Although Fr. Domingo Navarrete's criticisms of the Portuguese in general and of the Macaonese in particular were not always justifiable, there is no reason to doubt the accuracy of his assertion regarding the Convent of the Poor Clares at Macao that 'the foundation was made without His Majesty's leave and he resented it when it came to his ears; and not without reason, for a country of Infidels, and so small a footing is not proper for Nuns'. Nor was his comparison of the two cities, Manila and Macao, on the opposite shores of the South China Sea, altogether wide of the mark. Macao, he wrote, 'throve so much with the trade of Japan and Manila, that it grew vastly rich, but never would vie with Manila, nor is there any comparison between the two cities for all their analogies. I find as much difference, in all respects betwixt them, as is betwixt Madrid and Vallecas [much the same as between London and Hammersmith, adds his eighteenth-century English translator], and somewhat more, for the people of Manila are free, and those of Macao slaves to the Chinese.'[1]

Manila, which had a substantial number of European and Creole women, was better provided with Retirement Houses and with schools for girls than was Macao. The oldest was the House or College of Santa Potenciana, founded in 1594. Morga thus described it in his *Sucesos* of 1609: 'It is a royal foundation and the Prioress lives there with her confidential assistants. They admit women in distress, and maidens of the city, to a sort of religious retirement. Some of the girls leave there to marry, others remain there permanently. The institute has its own workrooms and a choir, partly maintained by royal grant; the rest they find for themselves by their own labour and from their property. They have their own steward and a chaplain who acts as administrator.'[2] In 1617–19, there was some correspondence between the Crown and the authorities at Manila over the grant of an *encomienda* to Santa Potenciana, since the actual income was insufficient. There were then four classes of women and girls who were admitted.

1. The daughters of impoverished old *conquistadores* and soldiers, who had been left destitute on their fathers' deaths.

---

[1] *Travels and Controversies of Friar Domingo Navarrete*, O.P. (ed. 1962), pp. 262–3.

[2] Antonio de Morga, *Sucesos de las Islas Filipinas* (ed. and trans. J. S. Cummins, Hakluyt Society edition, Cambridge, 1971), p. 285.

2. The illegitimate daughters of Spaniards and Indian (Filipina) women, 'and they are numerous'.

3. Some married women who had quarrelled with their husbands and who took refuge there until the marital discord was smoothed over.

4. Some poor but respectable widows.

At this period there were no separate quarters for women and girls, owing to the lack of money.[1]

Four years after the institute had opened its doors, there were some sixty girls there; but when Gemelli-Careri visited Santa Potenciana almost exactly a century later (May, 1696) he described it as 'a monastery or rather hospital [actually, College], founded by the King for sixteen poor orphans, to whom he allows a competent maintenance, and a portion when they marry. Married women are also admitted, and lewd women put in by the magistrates, but they have no communication with the sixteen orphans. The whores are maintained by the king, and they are to work for him. The church has three decent altars.' This College still existed in 1736, when the free inmates were described as being the daughters of Spaniards in the service of the Crown.[2]

This institution was supplemented in 1632–3 by another College called Santa Isabel, which was founded by the Manila branch of the Santa Casa da Misericórdia. Fr. Domingo Navarrete described it in his day as 'a stately church of the Misericórdia, with a school, in which they breed up many Spanish fatherless maids, and give them portions to marry. The best sort of inhabitants of Manila look after this Seminary; to be first-Brother of the Misericórdia is one of the chief posts in that government.'[3] Santa Isabel clearly became more favoured and consequently better endowed than the older Santa Potenciana. It was described in 1736 as being 'the house and seminary of Santa Isabel, built in order to rear Spanish orphan girls with thorough instruction in Christian doctrine and good morals ... Thence the girls go out with dowries sufficient for the

---

[1] E. H. Blair and J. A. Robertson, eds., *The Philippine Islands, 1493–1898* (55 vols., Cleveland, Ohio, 1903–09), vol. XVIII, *1617–1620*, pp. 282–8.

[2] G. F. Gemelli-Careri, *A Voyage round the World* (ed. 1744), p. 408; Blair and Robertson *The Philippine Islands*, vol. XLV, *1736*, pp. 254–7.

[3] *Travels and Controversies of Friar Domingo Navarrete, O.P.*, (1962 ed.), p. 94.

estate of marriage to which they naturally tend, for which purpose the Santa Casa has appropriated 16,000 pesos . . . It is a Seminary of such great reputation and honour that although it has been used from its beginning as a refuge for girls—the daughters of poor Spaniards whom the Brothers of the Misericórdia obtain from various houses and from Santa Potenciana—the best citizens of the community do not hesitate today to send their daughters there. Thence they go out to assume the state of matrimony, or as nuns of St Clare.' Their rich church was used as the cathedral until 1662.[1]

In addition to the two female Colleges of Santa Potenciana and Santa Isabel, there were various *beaterios* or Retirement Houses for pious women in Manila, including one, San Sebastian of Calumpay, founded for Filipina girls in 1719.[2] Some Spanish women, usually widows, also received *encomiendas* of Filipino Indians to help support them. There were complaints in 1599 that some 'aged women, mistresses of *encomiendas*', were marrying very late in life, just to ensure that the husband should succeed to his wife's *encomienda*. Governor Perez Dasmariñas had suggested that the marriage of such elderly ladies should be prohibited by law. But the scrupulous Philip II, while recognising that the abuse existed, ordered that 'no innovation should be made, restricting the liberty of such women to marry whom they wished'. A later decree stipulated that for a husband or wife to inherit the *encomienda* of a deceased spouse, they must have been married for at least six months.[3] Gemelli-Careri noted a century later that *encomiendas* in the Philippines were usually given for two lives, 'the wife and children succeeding in them,' after which they reverted to the Crown.[4]

Although Spanish women in this remotest outpost of empire were apparently well provided for, occasional scandals did occur. The most sensational involved Doña Catalina Zambrano, the young and flighty wife of the Governor Don Alonso Fajardo. She was carrying on an affair with an ex-Portuguese Jesuit from Coimbra, João de Messa, 'who had been expelled from the Society after having been

[1] Blair and Robertson, *The Philippine Islands*, vol. XXVIII, *1637–1638*, pp. 123 8.

[2] Ibid., vol. XLV, *1736*, pp. 259–62.

[3] *Cédula real* of 1599 *apud* José María Ots, *Instituciones Sociales de la America Española en el periodo colonial* (La Plata, Argentina, 1934), p. 117.

[4] G. F. Gemelli-Careri, *A Voyage round the World* (ed. 1744), p. 411.

a member of it for seven years, and who had subsequently been married three times, though he was not yet forty years old'. On the night of 11/12 May 1621, the Governor, accompanied by several soldiers surprised the guilty couple in Juan de Messa's house when they were going upstairs with an unnamed friend, 'a very noted pilot', just behind them. Fajardo ran the latter through with his sword, and the pilot staggered out into the street calling for confession, but was promptly killed by the soldiers. The Governor then attacked Juan de Messa, but as the latter was wearing a breastplate, he could only hit him in the throat and face, until finally Messa fell down the stairs and was finished off by Fajardo. 'During this struggle Messa was not heard to ask for confession, or even to say "Jesus" or any other words save only: "Whoever you are, don't kill me; consider the honour of your lady."' The Governor then sent for a priest to confess his wife in the room upstairs. 'The priest confessed her very slowly, taking more than half an hour. The Governor in the meantime was walking up and down.' When the confession was over, he killed his wife with a thrust through the heart. Her corpse was taken away soon after daybreak and buried in the Augustinian Church; but the bodies of her paramour and the pilot were left lying in the street all day, exposed to the gaze of a curious crowd of all nationalities, until some members of the Misericórdia removed them after nightfall and buried them in a common but unmarked grave. It has been suggested that Calderón drew on this real-life tragedy for the plot of his drama, *El Medico de su honra*, but most critics reject the suggestion. It may be added that the Governor was within his legal rights in killing his erring wife, since under Castilian law he had to kill both or else neither one of the couple caught *in flagrante delicto*.[1]

Another scandal with a happier ending occurred in the mid-eighteenth century when a strong-willed Dominican nun named Mother Cecilia fell in love with Don Francisco de Figueroa, Secretary to the colonial government. Although she had been a professed nun for sixteen years and despite the violent opposition of the Dominican friars, she insisted that her original profession was not valid and should be annulled. The case was eventually appealed to Mexico, but she resumed her maiden name of Cecilia

---

[1] This affair is fully documented from the original records in Blair and Robertson, *The Philippine Islands*, xx, *1621–1624*, pp. 34–43. For the legal position see José María Ots, *Instituciones Sociales*, pp. 350–1.

de Ita y Salazar and married Don Francisco at Manila before they sailed for Acapulco. The Archbishop of Mexico gave his decision in her favour and confirmed the validity of her marriage, as did the king by a royal decree of 1762, thus terminating a law suit which had lasted ten years since its inception.[1]

---

[1] Blair and Robertson, *The Philippine Islands*, vol. XLVIII, *1751–1765*, pp. 155–8. I owe this reference to Donna Vogt, Indiana University.

CHAPTER FOUR

The Cult of Mary and the Practice of Misogyny

In a handbook for the guidance and instruction of parish-priests, written by one of the most famous Augustinian missionary-friars in the Philippines and published at Manila in 1745, we find the following denunciation of women and all their ways:

'Woman is the most monstrous animal in the whole of Nature, bad-tempered and worse spoken. To have this animal in the house is asking for trouble in the way of tattling, tale-bearing, malicious gossip, and controversies; for wherever a woman is, it would seem to be impossible to have peace and quiet. However, even this might be tolerated if it were not for the danger of unchastity . . . Not only should the parish-priest of Indians abstain from employing any woman in his house, but he should not allow any of them to enter it, even if they are only paying a call.'[1]

This vitriolic outburst is typical of the strong stain of anti-feminine feeling which runs through so much of Iberian culture, social attitudes and literature in the period under consideration, although of course such sentiments were not confined to male Iberians. What Arnold Toynbee has termed 'the higher religions', and which I take to be (in alphabetical and not in pecking order) Buddhism, Christianity, Hinduism, Islam, and Judaism, all explicitly stress to a greater or lesser degree the natural inferiority of Woman and her lawful, right and proper subjection to Man. The traditional Chinese cosmogony, which revolves round the interaction of the *yang* (masculine) and the *yin* (female) elements, defines the former (light, active, generative essence) in more attractive terms than the latter (dark, passive, receptive essence), even if the term *yin* precedes *yang* when they are coupled together.

[1] Casimiro Dias, O.E.S.A., *Parrocho de Indios Instruido* (Manila, 1745), lib. I., cap. 2, fl. 14. But see Appendix V for a more balanced viewpoint by one of his contemporary Dominican colleagues.

7

'Woman is thy tilth; plough her as thou wilt' is one of the injunctions of the Koran. Ibn Mujavir, author of the *Tarikh Mustansiri*, a geographical treatise of *c.* 1226–42 A.D., in a chapter describing the then flourishing island-port of Quais in the Persian Gulf, states: 'At Quais the men are submissive to their wives and do nothing contrary to their wishes. But such an attitude does not conform to the Word of the Prophet, who said: "Consult them, but do just the opposite of what they say, for blessing is on him who opposes them."'[1] A slightly more tolerant but basically similar viewpoint was taken by Joseph Collet, an English Protestant Dissenter who was the Governor of Bencoolen in Sumatra nearly five centuries later. Defining his attitude to the local petty Indonesian rajahs, he wrote: 'I treat them as a wise man treats his wife, very complaisant in trifles, but immovable in matters of importance.'[2] Last, not least, we have Napoleon's opinion that a woman belonged to a man 'in much the same way that a gooseberry bush is the property of the gardener', a conviction which was reflected in Article 312 of the *Code Napoléon*.

Nothing would be easier than to pile up quotations from the literature and the correspondence of the sixteenth through eighteenth centuries which would reflect this conviction of innate masculine superiority, shared as it was, more often than not, by the women concerned, whether wives, widows, or daughters. Even such an avant-garde feminist (for her day and generation) as the Lady Mary Wortley Montagu, when unburdening herself to Bishop Burnet of Salisbury about the way in which men regarded women as being essentially stupid and petty-minded, added: 'I am not now arguing for an equality of the two sexes. I do not doubt God and Nature has thrown us into an inferior rank. We are a lower part of the Creation; we owe obedience and submission to the superior sex; and any woman who suffers her vanity and folly to deny this, rebels against the Law of the Creator and indisputable order of Nature.'[3] But here our concern is more narrowly focused on Iberian women and their menfolk overseas.

---

[1] In Arnold Wilson, *The Persian Gulf* (Oxford, 1928), p. 100.

[2] In H. Dodwell, *Private Letter-Books of Joseph Collett*, (London, 1933). This particular letter was written 12 September 1712.

[3] Lady Mary to Bishop Gilbert Burnet, 20 July 1710, in Robert Halsband, *The Complete Letters of Lady Mary Wortley Montagu* (3 vols., Oxford, 1965–7), vol. I, p. 45.

As noted previously, and as indeed is self-evident, the Iberian pioneers transported overseas the mental baggage which they had accumulated in the Peninsula. The conviction of feminine intellectual inferiority was one item in this baggage and it had the sanction of the highest and most respected authorities, including prominent theologians and luminaries of Holy Mother Church. Fr. Francisco de Vitoria O.P., revered as one of the founders of International Law and famous for his relatively humanitarian attitude to the Amerindians, had no doubt that women were intellectually and constitutionally unfitted to discuss spiritual and theological problems: 'Woman does not have spiritual knowledge, nor is it fitting that she should have. It therefore follows that she cannot discriminate in spiritual matters. And it would be a most dangerous thing to entrust the spiritual health of souls to a person who is incapable of distinguishing between what is useful or harmful for the good of souls.'[1] A viewpoint, incidentally, which would undoubtedly have commended itself to the New England Puritan divines who persecuted Anne Hutchinson.

Francisco de Vitoria's attitude was shared by some of his most distinguished colleagues. Indeed, some of them went further and argued that intense spiritual prayer and contemplation was dangerous and unnecessary for lay people in general and for the working-class in particular. The formidable Dominican, Melchor Cano, maintained that absorption in prayer would result in 'the cobbler sewing the shoe worse and the cook spoiling the meat'. Another Dominican, Fr. Alonso de la Fuente, wrote that lay persons should not give themselves to intensive prayer, because this involved such spiritual absorption 'that even if the woman saw her son fall into the fire she would not get off her knees to save him'. He added that prayer was not for married couples, and to teach them to pray intensively would be making a bed for heresies.[2]

Other anti-feminine and misogynistic writers whose works were widely read and presumably influential in this as in other respects, include Juan Luis Vives, author of the *Instruccion de la muger cristiana* (1555) and Baltasar Gracián, S.J. (1601–1658). The last-named in his celebrated *El Criticón* observed: 'Different kinds of

---

[1] Francisco de Vitoria, O.P., *Sobre la potestad de la Iglesia*, Releccion, 2nd ed., Biblioteca de los autores cristianos, p. 383.

[2] In J. S. da Silva Dias, *Correntes de Sentimento Religioso em Portugal, séculos XVI a XVIII*, vol. I, p. 444 n (Lisboa, 1960).

temptations make war on Man in his various ages, some when he is young and others when he is old; but Woman threatens him perpetually. Neither the youth, nor the adult, nor the old man, nor the wise, nor the brave, nor even the saint is ever safe from woman. This universal enemy is always sounding the alarm . . .'[1]

On a lower level, hagiographical lives of sixteenth- and seventeenth-century saints and holy men are often filled with details about how they were subjected to the wiles and temptations of the daughters of Eve and how they managed to resist them. We are often assured that such male paragons of piety and chastity would never look a woman in the face, but always kept their eyes on the ground when unavoidably forced to talk with one in public or in private. Even the saintly Xavier, who was more sensible in this respect, advised his subordinates to speak with women 'of whatsoever quality or condition they be', in public only, 'never going into their houses, save in case of extreme necessity, such as to confess them when they are ill'.[2]

Where the clergy led the way, the laity were not slow to follow. Anyone acquainted with Iberian literature of the sixteenth and seventeenth centuries will have no difficulty in recalling many examples of misogynistic writing. A few of these are collected in the work of P. W. Bomli, *La Femme dans l'Espagne du siècle d'or* (The Hague, 1950), and it would not be difficult to find many more.[3] It will suffice here to recall the *Carta de Guia de Casados* (Lisboa, 1651) of Dom Francisco Manuel de Mello, Portuguese on his father's side and Spanish on his mother's, as previously noted. His advice was not merely that men should lock up their daughters, but their wives as well. The latter should never appear at table if a man from outside the family came to dinner—nor in fact did they in Portugal, as we know from many travellers' accounts. If the wife brought a personal fortune to the marriage, she should give it all to her husband, even if she was legally entitled to keep it, 'for whoever gives a diamond ring [i.e. in this case the bride's virginity] naturally also gives the box in which it is enclosed'.

[1] Baltasar Gracián, S.J., *El Criticón* (originally published in 1651–7), *apud* Bomli, *La Femme dans l'Espagne du siécle d'Or* (The Hague, 1950), p. 164.

[2] Cf. St. Francis Xavier's 'Maneira para conversar com ho mundo pera evitay escandalos', April 1552, in G. Schurhammer S.J., and J. Wicki, S.J., *Epistolae S. Francisci Xaverii* (Rome, 1945), vol. II, pp. 431–3.

[3] Cf. pp. 154–75, *et passim*.

While not saying in so many words that women should be kept illiterate, Dom Francisco strongly advocated that their ability to read should be kept to the barest minimum—'the best book is the cushion and the embroidering-frame' (*o melhor livro é a almofada e o bastidor*).[1]

There was, admittedly, a cast of masculine thought which went the other way. Some avowedly pro-feminine works were published, which strove to defend women and to point out that in some respects at least they were (or could be) the equals of men. But this proto-feminist literature, if such it may be termed, was nothing like as influential as the contrary trend. Perhaps this was due, in part, to the fact that its practitioners tended to take all their examples from classical Greek and Roman models, neglecting the women of their own day and generation. For instance, the widely-travelled Cape Verdean physician, Cristovão da Costa, in his *Tratado en loor de las mujeres* (Venice, 1592) does not say a word about the women of Goa, Cochin and Macao, nor even of those of contemporary Spain and Portugal, but confines himself to the classical stereotypes of virtuous virgins and matrons.[2] The same is true of Diogo de Paiva de Andrade and his *Casamento Perfeito* (Lisboa, 1630). An earlier work on the same theme, *La perfecta casada* (1583) by the celebrated Spanish Augustinian friar, Luis de León (1527–91), is much more concerned with contemporary women; but he makes it crystal clear that Martha rather than Mary was the ideal at which to aim, and that women do not have the same spiritual potential as men. Duarte Nunes de Leão, the Portuguese chronicler (of New-Christian origin) whose *Descripção do Reino de Portugal* was published at Lisbon in 1610, does have three chapters devoted to the admirable qualities and achievements of Portuguese women in several fields. He discusses successively 'the honesty and retirement of Portuguese women and their perfections' in general; 'the valour and courage of Portuguese women', with examples taken from the sieges of Safim, Mazagão and Diu, etc., as well as Dona Guiomar, the jilted daughter of the Mathematician Pedro Nunes, who slashed her erstwhile lover across the face with a knife when both were

[1] D. Francisco Manuel de Mello, *Carta de Guia de Casados* (Lisboa, 1651), fl. 63. This little book was frequently reprinted, and translated into English by John Stevens, *The Government of a Wife* (London, 1697) with a highly commendatory preface to the reader.

[2] The identification of Cristovão da Costa, who published his works under the Spanish form of his name, Cristobal de Acosta, is due to Dr Francisco Guerra, M.D., the noted historian of Iberian Colonial medicine.

kneeling before the Bishop in a church at Coimbra; 'the capability of Portuguese women for letters and the liberal arts', in which he descants on the classical learning and erudition of the Infanta Dona Maria (daughter of King Manuel I), Joana Vaz, Luisa Sigea, and other cultured and accomplished court-ladies of the sixteenth century.[1] But these aristocratic ladies were swallows who did not make a summer; and his claim that Portuguese men were not in the least jealous or mistrustful of their women, and that the latter kept themselves closely secluded at their own desire, does not sound very convincing. His pro-feminine stance does not reflect the general attitude of Portuguese men of the gentry and *fidalguia*, which is more accurately mirrored in the anti-feminine *Tempo de Agora* of Martim Afonso de Miranda (2 vols., Lisboa, 1622–4) and the *Carta de Guia de Casados* of Dom Francisco Manuel de Mello (1651).

If the men tended to believe in the basic inferiority of their womenfolk in their home country, it is understandable that things were no better overseas, especially in societies which depended heavily on slave or on dirt-cheap labour. In the debate which raged at Goa in the 1590s over the desirability of establishing a convent of Nuns, as advocated by Archbishop Meneses, most of 'the many and grave Religious' who were asked for their opinions, originally voted against it. They argued 'that this sort of life was not suitable for the women of India, owing to their great weakness, the great luxury and delights of the land, the intemperance of the climate, and the licentious upbringing of the girls', exposed as they were to the baleful influences of a slave household.[2] In the end the Archbishop got his way, but it was several years before all doubts and misgivings were overcome and the Crown's reluctant consent finally obtained. On the other hand, those who were in favour of the Convent from the beginning, and the doubters who were subsequently converted, all agreed that a Convent of Nuns incarnated the highest form of female chastity and virtue, and would be of itself most pleasing to God. Clerical moralists never tired of

---

[1] Duarte Nunes de Leão, *Descripção de Reino de Portugal* (Lisboa, 1610), chapters 88–90. For the *dama da cutilada*, as Dona Guiomar was subsequently called, see also the contemporary narrative printed in Ernesto Donato (ed.), *Miscelânea* (Coimbra University Press, 1924), pp. 17–19. The lady became a Poor Clare at Coimbra after this escapade.

[2] In Germano da Silva Correia, *História da Colonização Portuguesa na India*, vol. II, p. 204.

eulogising virginity as superior to the married state for either sex, and they were equally fervent in advocating the cult of the Virgin Mary.

The Jesuit Alexandre de Gusmão (1629-1724), who spent most of his long life in Brazil, where he died as Rector of the Seminary of Belem at Cachoeira (Bahia) which he had founded in 1687, was the author of a work entitled *Arte de crear bem os filhos na idade de puericia* (Lisboa, 1685). In this substantial little book he expounds at length the virtues of 'the heavenly flower of virginity', and he explains that the best way of acquiring and retaining this sublime quality is to bring up children in the devotion of Our Lady. He states, no doubt correctly, that this was the reason why the Jesuits founded Congregations of the Virgin in their schools and colleges throughout the world, literally from Macao in China to Cuzco in Peru.[1] Padre Gusmão was, in this sense, preaching to the already converted, since the cult of the Virgin has always been extremely popular in the Iberian Peninsula, at least from the late fourteenth century. Both the Portuguese and the Spanish discoverers, pioneers, and *conquistadores* took this cult overseas with them and planted it firmly in all the regions where they settled for any length of time. They also introduced this cult to the converts whom their missionaries made in independent kingdoms and empires, such as China, Japan, Vietnam, and Moghul India. Very many—perhaps a majority—of the churches, hermitages, convents, and other pious establishments founded overseas were dedicated to Our Lady in one form or another (of the Rosary, of Sorrows, of the Snows, of the Assumption, etc. etc.) as for that matter were a majority of the Iberian ships. Inevitably the cult of the miraculous images of Our Lady flourished alongside these manifestations, giving rise to a vast hagiographical literature which has endured for centuries. One need only look, for example, at the section dealing with holy images in the historical bibliography compiled by Jorge Cesar de Figaniere over a century ago, although this refers merely to Portugal and its overseas possessions and is the tip of an iceberg.[2] Padre Rafael Bluteau, in a sermon preached in 1723, when enumerating

---

[1] Alexandre de Gusmão, S.J., *Arte de crear bem os filhos na idade de puericia*, p. 287. For this Jesuit pedagogue's attitude to the upbringing and education of girls, which was very much on the lines of 'lock up your daughters', see op. cit. cap. 25, pp. 377-87, 'Da especial cuidado que se deve na creaçam das meninas'.

[2] Jorge Cesar de Figaniere, *Bibliographia Historica Portuguesa* (Lisboa, 1850), pp. 256-61, 'Historias e Relações das Imagens que se veneram em Portugal, e

the sins and omissions of the citizens of Lisbon observed: 'Some people punctiliously keep all the Feastdays dedicated to Our Lady; but on Sundays, which are Our Lord's Days, many people work without considering it to be wrong.'

The popularity and fervour of the cult of the Virgin lost nothing in its emigration across the Seven Seas, and, if anything, tended to increase. Macao, for example, has been defined by one of its leading living historians as being and having always been the land of Saint Mary, 'a terra de Santa Maria'. Nor does Padre Manuel Teixeira have any difficulty in adducing facts and figures to prove this claim in his substantial and well-documented book, *O Culto de Maria em Macao* (Macau, 1969). The first church built there, which in due course became the cathedral, was dedicated to the Blessed Virgin Mary, as was the famous Jesuit Collegiate Church of Madre de Deus, and many of the other churches, chapels, and hermitages. Seven Marian confraternities for both sexes and all ages were founded by the Jesuits alone, and Marian festivals were celebrated with great splendour, fervour, and devotion. The original patron saint of Macao was Our Lady of the Conception (*Nossa Senhora da Conceição*, perhaps the most popular of all the Portuguese manifestations of Our Lady), to whom St John the Baptist, St Francis Xavier and St Catherine of Siena were subsequently added by the year 1646. Father Manuel Teixeira assures us that the historic image of Our Lady of the Conception was the only object which survived unscathed when Chinese Communist rioters wrecked and pillaged the building of the Municipal Council during three hours on 3 December 1966. A list of the surviving names of ships whose home-port was Macao likewise reveals a strong preference for Our Lady in one form or another. Several fortresses and some of the heavy bronze guns cast by the celebrated Bocarros at Macao in the seventeenth century were also called after the Virgin Mother of God. Stories and traditions of her miraculous interventions abound here as elsewhere in the Roman Catholic world; perhaps the most popular being her intervention on behalf of the City when a dangerous attack by the heretic Hollanders was beaten off on Midsummer's Day, 1622. Popular songs and folk-lore also contain many

suas Conquistas'. Cf. also Jacinto dos Reis, *Invocações de Nossa Senhora em Portugal d'Aquem e d'Alem Mar e seu Padroado* (Lisboa, 1967) and R. Vargas Ugarte S. J., *Historia del culto de María en Iberoamérica y de sus imágenes y santuarios más celebrados* (2 vols., Madrid, 1956).

Marian elements; and it would be interesting to compare them with those which have survived in Indonesia, Malacca, Ceylon, Goa, and in other places where once the Portuguese held sway in Asia.[1]

The popularity of the cult of Mary, 'Star of the Sea', at Macao is partly explicable by the parallel Buddhist cult of the Goddess of Mercy, Kwan-yin. She was also the Goddess of sailors and of the sea in some of her manifestations, including that of the local Goddess, Ama, to whom a small shrine existed at the time the Portuguese first came there.[2] Images of Kwan-yin, or Kwannon as she is called in Japan, often resemble those of the Madonna, as any collector of Chinese and Japanese porcelain knows. Hence the Japanese crypto-Christians, during the centuries when the Roman Catholic faith was strictly prohibited by the Tokugawa government (1614–1872), often used to worship the latter under the guise of the former, these images being known as Maria-Kwannon. Of course, there is nothing surprising or novel about this. The early Christian church often took care to found its sanctuaries on sites which had formerly been dedicated to heathen deities, thus facilitating conversion and continuity at the same time. The cult of the Virgin of Guadalupe, patron saint of Mexico, which is particularly popular with the indigenous inhabitants, certainly owed something in its early stages to the fact that the Virgin's miraculous appearance (in December 1531) occurred, and her church was subsequently built, at a place which had been sacred to the Aztec corn (maize) goddess.[3] The miraculous intervention of the Virgin at the battle of Midsummer's day at Macao in 1622, is paralleled by countless others in the Iberian colonial world. Some are mentioned by Bernal Diaz in his classic account of the conquest of New Spain— although, being a bit of a cynic, he remarks slyly that he was too much of a sinner to have actually seen these celestial apparitions

[1] Some of these were collected and published by H. Schuchardt in the *Zeitschrift für romanische Philologie* of Vienna in the last century, and others by Rodolfo Dalgado in various books and articles published at Goa, Lisbon, and elsewhere in the first three decades of the present century.

[2] Søren Egerod, 'A note on the origin of the name of Macao' in *T'oung Pao*, vol. XLVII (Leiden, 1959), pp. 63–6, has an interesting discussion but not, perhaps, the last word on this subject.

[3] George M. Foster, *Culture and Conquest. America's Spanish Heritage* (New York, 1960), pp. 207 n, 215.

himself.[1] António de Oliveira de Cadornega, the seventeenth-century Portuguese chronicler of Angola (p. 24 above) was more credulous (or more devout), for he relates several miraculous interventions of the Virgin Mary on the battlefield without expressing any doubt or qualification.

As indicated previously, the cult of the Virgin and her miraculous manifestations was certainly not limited to the poor and lowly, but was common to all ranks and conditions of men. We have seen it exemplified in the Mexican career of *La China Poblana* and we find it equally flourishing in Peru and in the Philippines. One of the most learned Jesuit writers at Manila in the eighteenth century, Padre Pedro Murillo Velarde (1696–1753), whose history of the Jesuits in the Philippines was published at Manila in 1749, dedicated this book to two of the most celebrated images of the Virgin in the Philippines. He had been chaplain to both their sanctuaries, at San Pedro Macati and at Antipolo, respectively, and he relates many miraculous occurrences concerning them.[2] At a much later date, it was with an image of the Virgin, which the Filipino patriot and national hero, José Rizal, had cherished in his student days, that the Jesuits sought to win him back to the church on the eve of his execution by a Spanish firing-squad (30 December 1896).[3] Nowadays, colonial baroque images of the Virgin are avidly sought by collectors the world over, but this does not alter the fact that they were once the objects of sincere and intense devotion, and in some places they still are.[4]

One of the most curious works exalting the cult of the Virgin is the *Luzeiro Evangelico* of an Italian Franciscan missionary-friar,

[1] Bernal Diaz del Castillo, *The True History of the Conquest of New Spain* (Hakluyt Society ed., 5 vols., London, 1908–16), vol. I, pp. 121–2, apropos of the alleged appearance of Santiago and San Pedro at the battle of Ciutla, 25 March (Lady Day), 1519.

[2] Pedro Murillo Velarde, S.J., *Historia de la Provincia de Philipinas, 1616–1716* (Manila, 1749), frontispiece and dedication. The shrine of the Virgin at San Pedro Macati contained what was alleged to be a hair of the Blessed Virgin Mary.

[3] Whether Rizal really retracted his agnosticism and reverted to Roman Catholicism is still hotly debated by his numerous biographers. For typical if opposing views on this point compare Austin Coates, *Rizal, Philippine Nationalist and Martyr* (London, 1968), and S. M. Cavanna y Manso, C.M., *Rizal's Unfading Glory* (2nd ed. Manila, 1956).

[4] Eduardo Etzel, *Imagens Religiosas de São Paulo. Apreciação Histórica* (São Paulo, 1971).

Giovani Batista Morelli, who had girdled the globe in the course of his travels in the late seventeenth and early eighteenth centuries. He wrote the book in Portuguese at São Tomé de Meliapor (now a suburb of Madras) on the Coromandel Coast of India in 1708; he dedicated it to a Spanish military officer at Manila in 1709; and it was published at Mexico City in 1710. I have only seen one copy, and I doubt if as many as half-a-dozen exist.[1] The book was written to fortify the faith of the Roman Catholic Eurasian communities at such places as Madras, Malacca, Batavia, Bengal and Ceylon etc., who were oppressed by their Calvinistic Dutch or other heretic overlords, or were exposed to the propaganda of the Danish and German Lutheran missionaries at Tranquebar. Morelli was a widely-travelled friar who had been in England in the year 1688, just before the Roman Catholic James II (who received him in audience) lost his throne to his Protestant daughter and son-in-law, the Prince and Princess of Orange; and for a short time he was a missionary in China. In the *Luzeiro Evangelico* he labours hard to defend the cult of saints and images from Protestant attacks, stressing that the cult was not rendered to the material of which the image might be made, but to the glory of God as manifested in the saint represented by the image. He emphasises that the cult of the Virgin is vastly superior to all others, since the Mother of God was also the quintessence of virginal purity and entitled to almost as much veneration as Christ himself, 'since after Jesus Christ there is not, nor can there be, another creature not only as great but even equal to her. And for this reason we owe her all the veneration, honour and worship which we give to all the Angels and Saints, but to her in a much greater degree. For in her alone, more than in all the others, shines the glory of the All-powerful and Most High God, in whom terminates all the worship which we render to her, as He is the fount of all the grace and glory which is in her.'[2]

---

[1] João Baptista Morelli de Castelnovo, O.F.M., *Luzeiro Evangelico que mostra a todos os Christãos das Indias Orientais o caminho unico, seguro, e certo da recta Fé, para chegarem ao porto de salvação eterna . . . obra de muita utilidade para os Ministros Christãos todos Catholicos, Protestantes doutos e indoutos . . . A devoção do Sargento-maior D. Francisco de Olaide, morador de Manila. Escrita em São Thomé, Cidade da India Oriental, Anno de 1708, e impressa em Mexico Cidade da India Occidental, Anno de 1710.* I have consulted the copy at the Public Library, São Paulo, Brazil. The only other one which I have been able to trace is in the Municipal Library at Peking.

[2] *Luzeiro Evangelico*, pp. 395–406.

The exaltation of female chastity and virginity, which was a common though not an invariable facet of the cult of the Virgin Mary, sometimes formed an obstacle to the complete and whole-hearted conversion of people and societies which did not place the same emphasis thereon. Padre José de Acosta, S.J., whose description of the New World and its inhabitants—more especially those of Peru—first published at Seville in 1590, immediately became a best-seller in several languages, is violently critical of the Amerindians in this respect.[1] 'However great and almost divine is the honour which all other peoples pay to virginity, these beasts consider it to be all the more despicable and ignominious.' He claims that no Peruvian man would think of marrying a woman without having had sexual relations with her for 'many days and months, and, shameful as it is to say it, nobody can make a good wife who has not previously been a concubine'. He claims that the missionaries had great difficulty in getting their Amerindian male converts to marry women who were still virgins, although their continual efforts to exalt the value of female pre-marital virginity were slowly bearing fruit.[2] Similar complaints came from other mission-fields as far apart as the Congo and Japan;[3] nor was the missionaries' task made any easier by the general attitude of many Iberian men. This has been (perhaps not altogether unfairly) summed up in the phrase that the women of one's own family were sacred but all others were fair game.

Fornicar no es pecada, 'fornication is no sin', or, in a slightly refined version, 'simple fornication is no sin' (presumably meaning fornication with an unmarried woman), was a widely held belief among Iberian—and many other—males in Padre José de Acosta's time and for long afterwards.[4] Acosta emphatically and unreservedly

[1] José de Acosta, S.J., *Historia Natural y Moral de las Indias* (Seville 1590), and his slightly earlier *De Procuranda Indorum Salute* (Salamanca, 1588), my quotations being taken from the Spanish translation of the latter by Francisco Mateos, S.J., *Obras del P. José de Acosta S.J.* (Madrid, 1954), pp. 389–608.

[2] Francisco Mateos, S.J., *Obras del P. José de Acosta S.J.* (1954), pp. 602–3.

[3] For the difficulties raised by Bantu polygamy in the old kingdom of Congo and in Angola, cf. Antonio Brásio C.S. Sp., (ed.), *Monumenta Missionaria Africana. Africa Ocidental*, vol. v, *1600–1610* (Lisboa, 1955), pp. 607–14. For Japan, cf. C. R. Boxer, *The Christian Century in Japan, 1549–1650* (ed. University of California Press, 1967), pp. 174–5; Jesús López Gay, S.J., *El Matrimonio de los Japoneses . . . segun Gil de la Mata S.J., 1547–1599* (Rome, 1964).

[4] For a typical example of this widespread attitude, dating from the Philip-

condemns clerical concubinage;[1] but we know from irrefutable sources that it was widely spread in Europe before the reforms instituted by the Council of Trent, and it certainly flourished in the colonial world for long after that.[2] The Jesuits had a far higher standard than most of the other Religious Orders in this as in other respects; and the worst offenders seem to have been the Peninsula and Creole secular clergy whose standards were often deplorably low. The Amerindian chronicler, Poma de Ayala (flourished, 1560–1615), leaves us in no doubt about the widespread concupiscence of many of the clergy in Peru, and his allegations are fully confirmed by other contemporary sources, including the records of the Inquisition.[3] With so many of the clergy comporting themselves like stallions, it is hardly surprising that many of the laity did likewise, although Francisco de Aguirre, the philoprogenitive conqueror of Chile (1500–1581), who boasted that he had sired fifty *mestizo* offspring in the twenty-three years which elapsed before his wife from Spain rejoined him, was clearly rather exceptional.

It need hardly be added that no such licence was allowed the Spanish and Creole women in the Indies, still less the Portuguese, unless they were prostitutes, and such were relatively rare, for the reasons already explained. An Iberian woman who was the mistress of a man was expected to remain as faithful to him as if they were living in lawful wedlock, and it is virtually certain that the great majority behaved in this way. All the writers who dealt with women and marriage, whether pro- or anti-feminine, were united in agreeing that adultery and unchastity in the woman was a much more serious crime than in a man. Dr João de Barros in his

---

pines in 1612, see Carlos Quirino and Abraham Laygo (eds.). *Regésto Guión Catalogo de los documentos existentes en Mexico sobre Filipinas* (Manila, 1965), p. 112 (denunciation of Francisco Gonçalves, a Portuguese, 'por decir que la simple fornicación no es pecado'). For Spanish women accused of being witches, ibid., p. 97.

[1] *De Procuranda Indorum Salute, apud* F. Mateos, S.J., *Obras Completas*, p. 418.

[2] Cf. The examples adduced by A. H. Oliveira Marques, *Daily Life in Portugal in the late Middle Ages* (Madison, 1971), pp. 175–8, and by José Sebastião da Silva Dias, *Correntes de Sentimento Religioso em Portugal, séculos XVI a XVIII*, Tomo I (Coimbra, 1960), pp. 33–66; Salvador de Madariaga, *The Spanish Empire in America* (New York, 1947), pp. 143–7, 356–7.

[3] Felipe Guamán Poma de Ayala, *La Nueva Cronica y buen gobierno* (ed. Luis Bustíos Gálvez, 3 vols., Lima, 1956–66), vol. II, pp. 185–8; Salvador de Madariaga, *The Spanish Empire in America*, pp. 143–7.

Espelho de Casados (Oporto, 1540), explained that if a wife is unfaithful to her husband, this afflicts him more than if his daughter had been deflowered, or his children had all died, or his property was all lost, or he himself was mortally wounded.[1] Just over a century later, Juan de Zabaleta' in his *El dia de fiesta por la mañana y por la tarde* (1654) stresses that there is no excuse for an adulterous woman, even if her husband has treated her very badly and has been chronically unfaithful. 'If he ill-treats her, let her bear it patiently, for either he will mend his ways or else she will become better still.'[2] The celebrated humanist Juan Luis Vives, in his *Instrucción de la mujer cristiana* (1555) states that adultery in a man is not so sinful as in a woman; for whereas a man leads a more active life and has to keep several values, a woman has only to guard her chastity.[3]

How far the colonial Iberian woman, whether Spanish or Portuguese, uncomplainingly accepted this 'double standard' of chastity as a natural fact of life, it is difficult to say. Many people with experience of Latin-America would probably agree with what William Lytle Schurz has written: 'Concubinage was not a phenomenon that ceases with the conquest. In spite of all the efforts of the Church and Crown to moralise the habits of the Spanish population, its popularity continued throughout the colonial period, to the greater increase of the mestizo population and the added demoralisation of customs. In fact, it has remained an accepted feature of Latin-American society, though surrounded by a certain protocol that mitigates its effects on family life.'[4] Similar arguments have been advanced in respect of Macao and Brazil; and it is obvious that the prevalence of concubinage did not, as a rule, lead to the break-up of the legitimate family, whatever resentment the lawful wife may secretly have nursed. This was, equally obviously, due to the indissoluble nature of the bond conferred through the sacrament of marriage by the teaching of the Roman Catholic Church. The

---

[1] Dr João de Barros, who should not be confused with his more celebrated namesake (likewise a *Minhoto*), the chronicler of the *Decadas da Asia*, cited by Edward Glaser, *Estudios Hispano-Portugueses. Relaciones literarias del Siglo de Oro* (Valencia, 1957), p. 89 note (51).

[2] Juan de Zabaleta (1626–1667), *El dia de fiesta por la mañana y por la tarde* (1654), *apud* Bomli, *La Femme dans l'Espagne*, p. 74.

[3] Juan Luis Vives, *Instrucción de la mujer cristiana* (1955), *apud* Bomli, *La Femme dans l'Espagne*, p. 74.

[4] W. L. Schurz, *This New World* (London, 1956), p. 65.

Japanese aphorism that a woman has three lords during her life: her father (when she is unmarried), her husband (when she is married), and her son (when she is a widow), cannot be applied without qualification to the position of women in Iberian colonial society, where wealthy widows could play a positive role. Despite the inheritance laws which normally gave female children the same share of the inheritance as the male, Spanish and Portuguese law, in effect, only recognised the full legal capacity of women, other than widows, in exceptional circumstances. Unmarried women were normally subordinated to the authority of the father, the elder brother, or the nearest male relative, and a married woman to that of her husband.[1] But then so they were the world over, save for a few exceptional societies such as the Nairs of Malabar.

Spanish writers of the calibre of Salvador de Madariaga and Gregorio Marañón emphasise that the woman is normally perfectly content with her subordinate position: 'The two sexes keep to their original and natural roles . . . However wilful, capable and energetic —and Spanish women are often all three—women accept as a matter of course, nay, as a matter of nature, the supremacy of the male. There is in all this nothing but instinctive fidelity to natural laws.'[2] Maybe so; but perhaps the teaching and authority of the Church were more effective in making women content with (or at any rate resigned to) their lot than 'instinctive fidelity to natural laws.' After all, as Lady Mary Wortley Montagu admitted to her daughter in her old age, and in contradiction to the line she had taken with Bishop Burnet in 1710: 'I am inclined to think (if I dare say it) that nature has not placed us in an inferior rank to men, no more than the females of other animals, where we see no distinction of capacity, though I am persuaded if there was a commonwealth of rational horses (as Dr Swift has supposed) it would be an established maxim among them that a mare could not be taught to pace.'[3]

If the Church, as I have suggested, was the main factor in inducing the Iberian woman to accept the double standard in sexual

[1] José María Ots Capdequí, *Instituciones Sociales de la America Española en el periodo colonial* (La Plata, Argentina, 1934), pp. 205–6.

[2] Salvador de Madariaga, *Englishmen, Frenchmen, Spaniards* (London, 1928), p. 224; for Marañón's views see the extracts from his collected works and the comments by K. S. Reid in the *Bulletin of Hispanic Studies*, vol. XLVII (1970), p. 275.

[3] Lady Mary to Lady Bute, 10 March 1753, in R. Halsband, *Complete Letters*, vol. III, p. 25.

relationships more or less uncomplainingly, there are some indica-
tions that women were not invariably passive and uncomplaining
about it. Given the secrecy involved by the seal of confession we
are unlikely to learn anything much from that institution, which
would otherwise be the most obvious source. But it is significant
that St Francis Xavier in his previously quoted instructions of 1548
found it necessary to impress on his subordinates: 'You should
never blame the husband in public, even if he is the guilty party,
because the women are so bold that they seek opportunity to deni-
grate their husbands, telling Religious persons that the husbands
are the guilty ones and not they themselves.' He added that even
innocent wives should be urged to bear uncomplainingly with their
husbands' infidelities, 'inciting them to humility and patience, and
obedience to their husbands'.[1] Obedience to the husband by the
wife was something which clerical moralists never failed to stress
in or out of season. Fr. Luis de Granada, O.P., writing to the
Marchioness of Villafranca, Vicereine at Naples in 1587, in reply
to her request for guidance to married women, told her that in the
event of her wifely jealously being aroused, this was best removed
'by patience, by hearing masses, and by giving alms to the poor'.[2]

Whatever the complaints made by the ladies of Goa about their
unfaithful spouses in St Francis Xavier's day and generation, I
suspect that a more typical reaction was that of the peasant women
of the Alto-Minho in this century. They almost invariably remain
faithful to their emigrant husbands, even when the latter are absent
for many years on end, but they do not expect their men to behave
in the same way.[3]

[1] 'Maneira pera conversar com ho mundo pera evitar escandalos', d. Goa,
April 1552, in G. Schurhammer, S.J., and J. Wicki, S.J., *Epistolae S. Francisci
Xaverii aliaque eius scripta*, 11, *1549–1552* (Rome, 1945), pp. 431–2.

[2] Autograph letter of Fr. Luis de Granada, O.P., to the Marquesa de
Villafranca, d. Lisboa, 17 October 1587 (writer's collection).

[3] Colette Callier, 'Soajo, une communauté feminine rurale de l'Alto-Minho',
in *Bulletin des Études Portugaises*, Tome 27 (Lisboa–Paris, 1966), pp. 268–9.

Grant of an *encomienda* by Pedro de Valdivia, the pioneer Conquistador of Chile, to his mistress, Doña Inés Suárez, 1544

Valdivia explains the reasons for this grant, which implicitly contradict his characterisation of Doña Inés as a weak and frail woman. In point of fact, she yielded in toughness and endurance to no man, but by Hispanic convention she had to be described as physically frail and retiring.

'Vos, Doña Inés Suárez, venistes conmigo a estas provincias a servir en ellas a su Majestad, pasando muchos trabajos y fatigas, así por la largueza del camino como por algunos reencuentros que tuvimos conindios y hambres y otras necessidades que antes de llegar adonde se pobló esta ciudad [Santiago de Chile] se ofrecieron, que para los hombres eran muy asperas de pasar, cuanto más para una mujer tan delicada como vos, y más de esto, en el alzamiento de la tierra y venida de los indios a esta ciudad, que pusieron en término de llevársela, y vuestro buen esfuerzo y diligencia fué parte para que no se llevase, porque todos los cristianos que en ella habia tenían que hacer tanto en pelear con los enemigos, que no se acordaban de los caciques que estaban presos, que era la causa principal a que los indios venían a soltarlos, y vos, sacando de vuestras flacas fuerzas esfuerzo, hiciestes que matasen los caciques, poniendo vos los manos en ellos, que fué causa que la mayor parte de los indios se fuerse y dejasen de pelear viendo muertos a sus señores; que es cierto que si no murieran y se soltaran, no quedara un español vivo en toda esta dicha ciudad, y los demás que en esta tierra había con mucho trabajo fueron parte para se poder sustentar en ella, y después de muertos los caciques, con ánimo varonil saliste a animar a los cristianos que andaban peleando, curando a los heridos y animando a los sanos, diciéndoles palabras por esforzales, que fué mucha parte, con las que les decíades, fuesen adonde estaban hechos fuertes mucha cantidad de indios, muchas veces, e a la oración desbaratados, y desta venida que vinieron los dichos indios a esta ciudad os llevaron cuanto teníades sin dejaros ni ropa ni otra cosa, en que perdiste mucha cantidad de oro ye plata . . ."[1]

---

[1] From the extract in José María Ots, *Instituciones Sociales de la America Española en el periodo colonial* (La Plata, Argentina, 1934), pp. 236–7. For Valdivia and Inés Suárez see F. A. Kirkpatrick, *The Spanish Conquistadores* (London, 1926), pp. 272–87.

The Rape of Dona Margarida de Mendonça, 1611

In 1611, Dona Margarida de Mendonça sent the following petition to the Crown, alleging that she had been raped by Nuno da Cunha, a prominent *fidalgo* at Goa, who had sworn on a missal and a crucifix that he would marry her, which he subsequently refused to do. She and her mother petitioned the King to compel Nuno da Cunha to marry her. The Crown ordered the Viceroy secretly to investigate the complaint, and to persuade Nuno da Cunha to marry Dona Margarida if her allegations were justified. I am not certain what the eventual outcome was, but Nuno da Cunha seems to have been unmarried when he died at Sena as Governor of Moçambique in 1623.

Petição de Dona Margarida de Mendonça

Diz Dona Margarida de Mendonça, mulher fidalga, donzela, que ella estava em companhia de sua mãe Anna de Andrade com muita honra e recolhimento, e tida em muita reputação, como he notorio a toda esta corte e todas as religiões e fidalguia e á mais gente. N'este anno de 611 entrou hum dia Nuno da Cunha em casa de minha mãe, dizendo queria casar comigo, e concertando-se a haver de ser em segredo, esperando alguns dias ao diante, mas por ora se queria juramentar; n'uma ermida dentro n'huma capella com hum missal e hum Christo se juramentou commigo e fez voto, e alli sobre as chagas de Christo me recebeu por sua mulher, dizendo era christão e não haver mister mais testemunhas, pois elle era hum fidalgo de bem e temente a Deos: e nas mesmas horas, não querendo esperar tempo, se entregou de mi e me forçou; gritando eu, me deu e me rompeu o fato, dizendo era eu sua mulher, e se gritasse, me mataria às punhaladas, se fallasse ou aqueixasse a algũa justiça nem secular nem ecclesiastica; ao que me salteavam as casas todas as horas com forças, mandando hum cafre seu, que he o seu governo, pòr-me as adagas no rosto, que o não accusasse em cousa nenhuma; pelo que Senhor me ficou algum fato em seu poder, e assim mais me cortou hũa gadelha de cabellos, que em seu poder tem, e outras cousas, que tudo me tomou; er assim mais me fez fazer á força hum papel de condições como elle quiz, trazendo a nota de sua casa, e quando o não fizesse, me houvera logo de matar; e assim peço pelas chagas de Christo e pelos meritos da Virgem sua Mãe a Vossa Magestade me faça justica de tal força, prostrando-me nos pés de Vossa Magestade, dando querela do tal forçador, pedindo me faça Vossa Magestade justiça, justiça, justiça como rey e imperador que sois, pois senhor estaes na terra por rey, e justiça para que elle case comigo.[1]

[1] R. A. de Bulhão Pato (ed..), *Documentos Remettidos da India ou Livros das Monções,* Tomo II (Academia Real das Sciencias de Lisboa, 1884), pp. 443–4. On p. 442–3, a covering letter from the Crown (the Bishop Dom Pedro de Castilho and the Count-Admiral of Vidiguerira), d. Lisbon, 28 March 1613, ordering the Viceroy, Dom Jerónimo de Azevedo, secretly to investigate the allegations, 'through a Religious of great authority and virtue who is not a friend of any of the parties involved'. Another, shorter, letter to the same effect in ibid., op. cit., p. 413.

APPENDIX III

An Iberian misogynistic jingle of *c*. 1614

This curious jingle was recorded by Pieter van den Broecke, a Dutchman of Flemish origin, who traded on the West African coast (1605–14) and in Asian lands and seas (1614–40). Whether he picked it up in Europe, Africa, or Asia, I cannot say; but I have not been able to trace the original.[1]

> Casete, mij hijo
> no quiere casarme
> Casate mij hijo
> no quiere casarme
> mas quiero ser libre que no cativarme.
>
> No me casaria
> con viuda por cierta
> tendome en la cama
> suspira por muerta
> este disconcerto solo para matarme
> mas quiere ser libre que no cativarme.
>
> No me casaria
> con donsella povre
> que tinga virtude
> hasta que le sobre
> A agua salobre piense saltarme
> mas quiere ser libre que no cativarme.
>
> No me casaria
> con mosa soldada
> tien malas costumbres
> Y mal ensonada
> parida y enprenada no puede escaparme
> mas quiere ser libre que no cativarme.

[1] K. Ratelband, *Reizen naar West Afrika van Pieter van den Broecke, 1605–1614*. vol. 52 of the Linschoten-Vereeniging series, The Hague, 1950, p. 94.

APPENDIX IV

Bequests for the girls and *mui-tsai* of Macao, 1614

The testator, Christovão Soares, was evidently a wealthy man with no children of his own, judging by these numerous bequests to girls described as *afilhadas* (god-daughters), and as slave-girls (*moças*).

'*Verbas condicionães do deffuncto Christovão Soares.*

Deixo a filha de Rafael de Almeida minha afilhada 50 pardaos, e se morrer fiquem à sua Irmãa.

A hũa filha de Sebastião Fernandez, a mais velha, deixo 50 pardaos. A qual he cunhada de Antonio de Pina, e se morrer fiquem à primeira Irmãa sua depois della, e depois às outras.

A hũa filha de Jorge Serqueira, minha afilhada, deixo 50 pardaos, e se morrer fiquem à outra.

A Violante, filha de João Fernandez e de Maria Pires, que está em casa de Jorge Serqueira deixo 50 pardaos, e se morrer antes de cazar fiquem à minha afilhada filha de Jorge Serqueira, e morrendo ella à outra Irmãa; e não quero que sua may tenha parte neste dinheiro porque me tem custado de duas naos e hum junco, que lhe tinha dada trezentos e 90 taeis que todos se perderão do emprego que lhe dey.

Declaro que à Orphãa Violante minha afilhada, que está em casa de Jorge Serqueira, tenho dada para mandar a Jappão hum pico de seda, na qual seda tem ella jà por sua conta quarenta taeis que eu lhe dey; e ademais jà lhe empresto outra vez, para mandar a Jappão este anno que vem de 1614, donde trazendo Nosso Senhor a salvamento lhe darão os ganhos de hum pico de seda a 40 taeis com que ella entrou, e eu lhe dei o anno passado, e a demazia, mando que se arrecade. E se Nosso Senhor a levar por sy, em tal cazo quero que fique esta esmolla à filha de Jorge Serqueira, minha afilhada, como jà acima digo.

Declaro que a Madalena atras, que deixava a Pedro Soares e a sua mulher Sicilia da Cunha, que servisse 8 annos, pois Deos foi servido levar para si Sicilia da Cunha, a tenha posta em casa de

Maria Soares mulher de Gaspar Correa, e lhe deixo que a sirva 6
annos, e depois cazará com hum homem da terra, ou o que lhe bem
parecer dando lhe primeiro a sua carta de alforria, para que lhe deixo
mais fora dos 20 pardaos que atraz digo, meyo pico de seda, e meyo
cate de seda de Sypeo[1] de quatro cestos, que agora mando para
Jappão, e o dinheiro que se fizer no cesto se entregará a Pedro
Soares, com os mais 20 pardaos que atras digo para que os arrisque
para India e Jappão para se poder cazar, e lhe peço que olhe para
ella, e sendo cazo que Deos faça algũa cousa a Gaspar Correa,
mando que a dita moça se entregue a Belchior Fernandez e a Isabel
Goncalvez minha comadre, sua mulher, com os mesmos seis annos,
e que olhem para ella por amor de Deos, e a Santa Casa da Misericordia peço pelo amor de Deos que tãobem olhe para ella, pois não
tenho nenhum outro, e sendo cazo que a dita moça falleça, mando
que o que lhe deixo, se faça bem para minha e sua alma, e declaro,
que sendo cazo que Nosso Senhor faça algũa cousa de Pedro Soares,
mando que este dinheiro se entregue a Caza Santa de Misericordia,
para que o traga a ganhos para a dita moça, correndo o seu risco. As
quaes verbas condicionaes que por todas são seis, eu Francisco
Araujo Escrivam desta Santa Caza aqui tresladei tiradas do dito
testamento do deffunto Christovão Soares e do seu condicilio, a que
me reporto na Meza do despacho hoje 10 de Janeiro de 615. Francisco de Araujo.'[2]

---

[1] I cannot explain this word.
[2] Arquivo da Santa Casa de Misericórdia, Macao, Codice 15, fls. 18.

APPENDIX V

Filipina and Spanish women compared, 1689

Fray Bartolomé Marron, O.P., Circular letter addressed to the
Dominican province of the Holy Rosary, Philippines, 30th September 1689.
Some Dominicans complain of the temptations to which they are
subjected in the Philippines; but Fr. Marron thinks that they are
less than those suffered in Europe:

'... no puedo dejar de añadir un casso (a que me halle presente) por
ser de mucha edificacion. Estaban en una cassa de Manila unos
quatro o seis capitanes mozos en conversacion y uno de ellos
comenzó a dezir que era dificultosissimo en esta tierra guardar con-
tinencia por las occassiones que avia, con el qual concordaban todos
los otros, hablando del punto menos el dueño de la cassa, que tambien era mozo y soltero como las demas, y de virtud. El qual aviendo
oydo a todos tomo la mano y dixo: parece que se han olvidada, de
las ciudades, no solo en la Nueva España sino tambien en España la
vieja y en aquellos mesones, donde son infinitas las mugeres que
persiguen a los hombres especialmente si los ven de buen pelo y
no les dejan hasta que por varios caminos los corotrasten. Tanto
tiempo a que estoy en esta tierra como Vmds. y en ella no he visto
nada de lo que he visto en otras partes, ni a avido muger hasta agora
que aia hablado palabra conmigo buena, ni mala. Y assi entiendo
ue en esta parte es la mejor tierra esta, que ay entre Christianos.
Dexen Vmds, de inquietar a las mugeres que yo les asseguro que
ellas no les inquietaran. Esto dixo aquel seglar, y todos sabian que
hablava verdad en lo que dezia de si. Y tambien en lo que dezia de
las mugeres hablava verdad que yo he oido a muchos hombres muy
experimentados dizir, que acqui las mugeres nunca inquietan a los
hombres, Y como persuadir a hombre alguno de razon, que una
india inquiete a un español y mas sacerdote! Algunas cassos abran
sucedido, pero muy raros.
Source: Archive of the Dominicans, Manila, Convento de Santo
Domingo. I owe this extract to the courtesy of my friend and
colleague, Professor J. S. Cummins.

APPENDIX VI

Autograph letter of advice from the Countess of Assumar to her son, Dom Pedro de Almeida, dated 2 June 1704

All students of Iberian history know how extremely rare is private correspondence of this type. It is true that the Countess of Assumar, *née* Dona Isabel de Castro, was never overseas, so far as I know; but the son to whom she addressed such sound advice, later made his mark as Governor of Minas Gerais in Brazil (1717–21) and as Viceroy of Portuguese Asia in 1744–50, after serving with credit in the War of the Spanish Succession, 1704–1713.

'Meu Filho a preciza obrigação em que o perceito de Sua Magestade que Deos guarde, pos a vosso Pay de acompanhar, e de assistir a El Rey Catholico, lhe não tem premetido que ellse fosse dos primeiros que pegaçe nas armas, e que viceis hir para as Frontieras; e como elle não pode aparesser nellas se não ao paço em que forem as Magestades não consente o seu brio (e tãobem por condecender com o vosso dezejo) que estejaes ociozo na Corte, quando temos na campanha jà, o nosso exercito, nem tão pouco que pello interesse da sua companhia vos dilateys em ter parte na gloria que esperamos em Deos consigão as nossas armas.

E como esta he a primeira ves que vos separais da caza e da assistencia de vosso Pay me acho eu obrigada pello amor que sempre me soubestes merecer, e pello cuidado com que athe agora me apliquei a vossa educação, a fazeruos algũas advertencias, fiando de vos que paçareis pellos olhos este papel algumas vezes, com aquella attenção que vos merece hũa May que com o mayor affecto, mais a vos que a qualquer outro filho, vos dezeja ver hum prefeito cavalhero.

Mas para o seres he necessario que tinhaes entendido que nem com aquelle caracter, nem com o de bom soldado, tem nenhũa incompatebilidade o ser bom catholico, antes sem esta condição, não podereis conceguir nem hũa, nem outra: assim a primeira couza a que vos aveis de aplicar, he a não perder a costume em que vos tenho posto de ouvires missa todos os dias, e de não faltares em nenhum por mayores que sejão as vossas occupações, em rezar o oficio de Nossa Senhora de quem vos encomendo muito que sejais enfenitamente devoto, porque siguros tereis os vossos acertos, e as vossas felicidades, debaixo do seu amparo, e da sua protecção, e tãobem vos confeçareis nos seus dias, e o mais ameudo que vos for possivel; nem entreis em acção arriscada sem que primeiro tinhaes feito esta deligencia, porque hireis aos perigos tanto mais animozo, quanto melhor na conciencia andareis ajustado.

Não mormureis de ninguem, nem digaes grassas que possão pezar, porque não ha peçoa de tão caleficado porcedimento nem de tão abalizadas vertudes a que os emulos, e os escandelizados não possão arguir de dous mil defeitos, e se não quizeres que vos ponhão na prassa os vossos, procurar encobrir os alheyos.

Nao sejaes de nenhũa maneira desconfiado porque he viceo perigozissimo em hum cavalhero mosso, porque não só aos Amigos sereis pezado, mas offendereis o vosso mesmo brio se entenderes que ha peçoa que possa deslustralo.

Ja sabeis que nunca vos consenti que juraceis, agora vos torno a advertir que o não faraes porque do contrario fareis escrupuloza a vossa verdade, desgrassa a mais lamentavel em hum homem branco.

Não peçais dinheiro emprestado porque bem tendes conhecido do animo de vosso Pay, e do cuidado que tem, de que vos não falte nada, que ao menor avizo tereis logo o socorro para tudo o que vos for necessario, mas se acazo tiveres hum tal aperto que não sofra esta dilação e que vos seja percizo valer de algũa peçoa, não ponhais prazo breve ao vosso dezempenho, porque se não de cazo que falteis a vossa palavra, e procuraray promptamente dezempenhala, e adquerir openião de verdadeiro, e de pontual, e assim achareis mais facilmente quem em outras occaziões vos assista.

Ponde grande cuidado em ser amigo de todos em comum, e particularmente dos que tiverem mais valor, e mais vertude, porque estes vos poderão servir de exemplo, e ajudar com o seu conselho quando vos seja necessaria.

De nenhũa maneira pareçais soberbo com os inferiores, antes os favorecereis com bom modo, e com agrado em tudo o que poderes, nem vos femeliarizeis senão com os iguais a vos, porque de outra sorte, nem daquelles vos fareis respeitar, nem estes vos poderão ter em grande conta.

Vosso Pay vos manda assentar prassa, sigundo me disse quando

se foy, e ainda que seja totalmente alheyo da minha profição dar
documentos a hum soldado, o amor que vos tenho, e o dezejo dos
vossos acertos, espero que mudem, a que transformem de tal sorte
as paixões femenis em affectos marciaes, que adoutrina de hũa
molher possa concorrer para vos constetuir hum perfeito cappitão,
e hum verdadeiro netto de tantos avos que de hum e outro apellido
Almeydas e Mascarenhas[1] ennobrecerão jà com as suas façanhas as
nossas historias, advertindo que a grandeza adquerida he muito
mais glorioza que a herdada porque naquella so teve parte a fortuna,
e esta conseguece so pelo proprio merecimento.

Isto suposto tende entendido que os primeiros paços que hum
homem da no mundo são os que canonizão ó os que distrõem a sua
opinião, assim ponde todo o vosso cuidado em regular as vossas
acções com tanto acerto que desde o prencipeo nos possamos pro-
meter a gloria com que daqui a enfenitos annos aveis de acabar todas
as vossas, para cujo fim concorrera muito procurares imitar a vosso
Pay, cujas vertudes paço em silencio, não por temer parecervos
sospeita, mas porque dellas fostes sempre cuidadoza testemunha.

Desde o dia que assentares prassa assentay tãobem com vosco que
a obrigação de hum bom soldado consiste em hũa cega obediencia
às ordens dos seus cabos, porque quem não sabe obedecer nunca
saberá bem mandar, e assim não replicareis a nenhũa, nem deixareis
de seguir todas as que vos forem dadas, e por mais ariscada que seja
a empreza para que vos destinarem hide com semblante alegre, e
com sosegado animo para que se não de cazo que chegue ninguem
a se preçoadir que os perigos vos fazem horror, nem a que sois tão
melindrozo que repugnaes ao trabalho, antes quanto elle for mayor
andareis mais dezaçombrado, e tende entendido que na campanha
não ha lugar seguro, e que coanto hum homem de bem se arisca
mais pello serviço da sua patria, pello seu Rey, e pella sua honra,
mais parece que obriga a Deos a que o defenda.

Não he isto querervos temerario porque tamanho viceo he em
hum soldado tirarce do seu posto por se preçoadir erradamente
que em outro do mais perigo poderá conseguir mais fama e mayor
nome, como deixar de hir para donde os seus cabos o tem assinado,
com o que não deixareis nunca o posto que vos tocar por nenhum
acontecimento porque do contrario nassc a confuzão c a dezordem
em que eu sentirey muito que vos tinhaes parte; alem de que

[1] Dona Isabel de Castro was the daughter of Dom João Mascarenhas, Marquis
of Fronteira and his wife Dona Margarida de Castro.

emquanto hides a outra empreza voluntario, tiver a vossa companhia acção, arrependervos-eis muito de que falte na lista dos que nella obrarão bem o vosso nome.

Se passares, como espero, a ter posto mayor examinay com toda aplicação, e com todo a cuidado, os seus encargos, e as suas obrigações, e nao falteis a nenhũa, e será muito conveniente ter pratica da fortificação, e das couzas pertencentes à Artelharia.

Sereis grande honrador dos soldados, e fazeilhes as boas passagens que poderes, sendo liberal com elles, e com todos, mas com tal porporção que a vossa generozidade não chegue a parecer desperdiçeo, porque nem a todos se deve dar pela mesma medida, mas deveis regularvos pella vossa obrigação, ó pella falta que souberes que elles tem.

Não ha couza mais natural na guerra que padecer dous mil discomodos, assim na falta do alimento para a vida, como na do descanço para o corpo, porque he muito ordinario andar por asperos caminhos, e esposto às inclemencias do tempo; porem quando chegue a suceder vos assim, peçovos que nem andeis triste, nem vos queixeis de cançado, porque isto he somente para homens vis e para animos abatidos, antes fazer boa cara ao trabalho, e mostray que vos alegrais com elle porque assim o fareis mais suave, e com o uzo vireis a não sentilo.

De nenhũa acção vossa, por mais que ella seja relevante vos aveis de jactar nunca, mas se vos for percizamente necessario falar nella, será com hũa tal modestia, que não a vos, senão a Deos atrebuais todo o bom suceço que tiveres, porque delle magnão todas as felicidades.

Suponho que vosso Pay vos manda encomendado ao Marques de Fontes para servires no seu terço, e para que as suas vertudes, que observareis com todo o cuidado, e para que o seu exemplo, que seguireis como o melhor modelo de todo o bom procedimento sejão as mais abonados fiadores dos vossos acertos; e assim deveis seguir sem escrupulo os seus dictames, e obedecer inviolavelmente aos seus preceitos, e não fareis nada sem o seu conselho ou sem a sua aprovação.

Mas estay advertido que quem vay para caza alheya deve por grande cuidado em não fazer de nenhũa sorte, pezada a sua companhia, a quem o honra tendo-o nella, assim procuray quanto estiver em vos granjear o seu agrado, e meresser o seu favor.

No comer não paressais melindrozo, mas asseitar o que vos

derem, e o seja mal, o bem sazonado, aveis de gabalo, e agradesselo quanto vos for possivel, para mostrares que de tudo vos contentays, e vos satisfazeis, e aos criados do Marques tratareis com afabelidade, e com bom modo.

Se tiveres algum tempo livre, não vos descudeis de abrir os vossos livros porque a applicação às letras, não embarassa o uzo das armas, antes mais ayrozo maneja estas, quem está mais senhor daquellas, e ainda que não faltarão curiozos, ou mal intencionados que vos digão, que não são de prova aquelles bacamartes para a campanha, entendey que para todos os lances as siencias são boas armas, e não vos deixeys esquesser do que tendes aprendido com tanto trabalho, poque estes conselheiros costumão ser muito sospeitosos.

E não entendais que por estares mais distante de vosso Pay lhe deixarão de chegar as noticias do vosso bom ou mão procedimento, assim espero de vos que vos aveis de portar de tal sorte que meressais que elle e eu vos deitemos muitas benções, e a de Deos vos cubra, e vos guarde muitos annos como direito. Lisboa em 2 de Junho de 1704

Vossa May que vos quer muito

Condessa de Assumar.'[1]

[1] Original autograph letter in the author's collection. I have kept the Countess's spelling, but made very occasional alterations in her rather erratic punctuation. She had a beautiful copper-plate hand, something rather unusual among ladies of her day and generation. Her son, to whom this letter was addressed, was born in 1688 and died in 1756. For a biographical sketch of him see my *Golden Age of Brazil, 1695–1750* (University of California Press, 1962), pp. 362–4.

ENGLISH ABSTRACTS OF THE IBERIAN DOCUMENTS

1. Reasons for the grant of an encomienda to Doña Inés Suárez by Pedro de Valdivia, Conqueror of Chile, 1544.

Addressing her in the first person, Valdivia recalls that Doña Inés had come with him to serve His Majesty in Chile, where the hardships and dangers 'were very rough for men to undergo, and how much the more for a delicate woman like you'. Her courage and presence of mind helped to save the city of Santiago from the rebellious Araucanians who were besieging it, and who had reduced it to dire straits. It was she who suggested killing the captive chiefs whom the besiegers were trying to rescue, 'laying hands on them yourself . . . gathering strength from your frail physique'. Their death disheartened the attackers, who retired defeated. She was also foremost in nursing the wounded and encouraging the defenders by word and example. The grant was made in partial compensation for the quantities of clothing, gold and silver, which she had lost in this rebellion.

2. The rape of Dona Margarida de Mendonça 1611.

Dona Margarida de Mendonça, an unmarried maiden lady, states that she was living quietly and respectably with her (widowed) mother, Anna de Andrade, as is well known to the Religious, gentry, and other inhabitants of Goa. One day in this year of 1611, Nuno da Cunha came to her mother's house and said that he wished to marry Dona Margarida, but that the actual ceremony would have to be celebrated secretly a few days later. All that he wanted to do then was to take a solemn oath in the chapel of a hermitage, swearing on a missal and with a crucifix that he received her as his wife, 'saying that there was no need for any other witnesses, because he was a Christian and an upright and God-fearing gentleman. And in that same hour, not wishing to wait any longer, he seized hold of me and raped me. When I began to scream, he beat me and tore my clothing, saying that I was his wife, and that if I screamed he would stab me to death; and he would do the same if I subsequently spoke about this or complained of it to any ecclesiastical or secular justice.' He later mistreated her gravely, entering her house at all hours to rob and abuse her, ordering his favourite Negro slave to put daggers to

9

her face, telling her not to accuse Da Cunha of anything. He also made her sign an irregular paper, which he had drawn up himself, under threat of death if she refused. She therefore begs the King in the name of the Virgin and the five wounds of Christ, to do 'justice, justice, justice, on this rapist', compelling him to marry her.

3. *Iberian misogynistic jingle of* c. *1614.*

Get married, my son/ I don't want to marry/get married my son/I don't want to marry/ I would rather be free than a slave.

I don't want to marry/ with a widow for sure/ for when I'm with her in bed/ she will sigh for the dead./ This alone would be enough to kill me/ I would rather be free than a slave.

I don't want to marry/ with a poor damsel/ who may have virtue/ enough and to spare./ I think that such salt water would salt me/ I would rather be free than a slave.

I don't want to marry/ with a soldierly wench/ who is badly behaved/ and worse taught./ Whether pregnant or in childbed I could not escape her/ I would rather be free than a slave.

4. *Bequests for the girls and* mui-tsai *of Macao, 1614. Conditional bequests of the late Christovão Soares.*

1. 50 *pardaos* to the daughter of Rafael de Almeida, 'my god-daughter'. And if she dies, they go to her sister.
2. 50 *pardaos* to the eldest daughter of Sebastião Fernandez, who is the sister-in-law of António de Pina. And if she dies, they go to the eldest surviving sister, and so on.
3. 50 *pardaos* to a daughter of Jorge Serqueira, 'my god-daughter, and if she dies, they go to the other'.
4. 50 *pardaos* to Violante, daughter of João Fernandez and Maria Pires, who is living in the house of Jorge Serqueira. 'If she dies before marrying, this sum goes to my god-daughter, the daughter of Jorge Serqueira; and if she dies, to her other sister'. The mother is not to have any share in this bequest, as the testator had already given her 390 taels' worth, all of which were lost in the cargoes of two ships and a junk.
5. A picul of silk is to be invested in Japan for another god-daughter, the orphan Violante, who is also in Jorge Serqueira's house, who has already had 40 taels on this account. If she dies, the bequest will be transferred to his other god-daughter, the daughter of Jorge Serqueira mentioned in (3) above.

6. The girl (obviously a *mui-tsai*) Madalena had been bequeathed to Pedro Soares and his wife Cecilia da Cunha, to serve them for eight years. As Cecilia da Cunha died before the expiry of this time-limit, the girl was transferred to the house of Maria Soares, wife of Gaspar Correa, where she is to serve for six years. She can then marry with a local man, or whoever she wants, being first given her certificate of manumission *(a sua carta de alforria)*. To help her in her future state of life, the testator now makes her some additional bequests in silk to be invested in the Japan trade. The proceeds from this and from previous bequests will be entrusted to Pedro Soares for reinvestment in the trade with India and Japan, 'and I ask him to look after her'. Should anything happen to Gaspar Correa, the girl is to be entrusted to the care of Belchior Fernandez and his wife Isabel Gonçalves, for the same period of six years. The testator implores both this couple and the Holy House of the Misericórdia to look after this girl. If she dies, the money is to be spent on masses for her and for the testator's souls. If anything should happen to Pedro Soares, the money is to be entrusted to the Misericórdia, to invest on her behalf and at her risk.

These six additional bequests were copied from the codicil to the last will and testament of the late Christovão Soares on the 16 January 1615 by Francisco de Araujo.

5. *Filipina and Spanish women compared, 1689.*

Fray Bartolomé Marron O.P. states that one day he was in a house at Manila conversing with some young officers, when one of them began to complain about the great difficulty of keeping chaste in this city. The others all agreed with him, save only their host, who was a young bachelor like them, but a virtuous one. Having heard them out, he intervened to say that they seemed to forget that in the cities of New Spain (Mexico) and Old Spain there were many women who tempted men and who would never leave them alone until they had entangled them. He added that he had been in Manila as long as the others, and he had seen nothing of this kind there, nor had he met any woman who had accosted him with either good or bad words. 'If you gentlemen will stop pestering the women, I guarantee that they will not pester you.' The friar applauds this young man's attitude, and claims that he spoke the literal truth.

'And can any intelligent man think that an Indian woman would tempt a Spaniard, and still more a priest! There have been a few such cases, but they are very rare.'

6. The Countess of Assumar's advice to her son when off to the war, 1704.

She begins by saying that since his father is absent, attending on the Catholic King (*i.e.,* The Archduke Charles of Austria, the Hapsburg claimant to the Spanish Crown), she has resolved to write her favourite son this letter with some advice, which she hopes he will keep and read attentively from time to time.

Above all, he should remember that there is nothing incompatible with being simultaneously a perfect gentleman, a good soldier, and a good Catholic. In fact, without being the last, he will not fully attain either of the other two. He must, therefore hear Mass daily, as she has brought him up to do, and likewise daily recite the office of Our Lady, whose protection will assure his happiness and success. He should also go to confession on her Holy Days, nor should he undertake any dangerous action before having done this, since the clearer his conscience, the braver he will be.

He must not gossip ill-naturedly about anyone, but should remember that even the most virtuous people are liable to be scandalously abused by jealous tongues. 'If you don't want your own faults to be noised abroad, you should try to conceal those of others.' He must not be mistrustful, for this is a very dangerous failing in a young gentleman.

She reminds him that she has never allowed him to swear, and she urges him emphatically to avoid doing so. This vice is bound to reflect on his own veracity, 'the most regrettable misfortune in a white man' *(desgrassa a mais lamentavel em hum homem branco).*

He should not ask for monetary loans, since his father has made him an adequate allowance and will send him more money whenever he needs it. However, if he does have to borrow money in an emergency, he should not promise to repay the loan within too short a time, as otherwise he may be unable to do so punctually and will lose his credit.

He should take care to be friendly with people in general, and particularly with the brave and the virtuous; because these will set him a good example and can give him good advice.

He should carefully avoid being arrogant towards his social inferiors. He should treat them affably and generously, while avoiding familiarity, which should be reserved for his equals.

His father has arranged for him to enlist in the army, and although as a woman she cannot tell a soldier how to behave, yet in the circumstances she feels that she must change her feminine feelings into martial ones, 'so that the instruction of a woman may help you to become a perfect captain and a worthy descendant of so many Almeidas and Mascarenhas who have ennobled Portuguese history with their exploits'. She adds that distinction earned on the battlefield is worth even more than that conferred by noble birth. He should imitate his father as far as possible.

From the day he enlists, he must realise that his first duty is a blind obedience to the orders of his superior officers, 'for whoever does not know how to obey will never make a good commander'. He must obey all orders cheerfully and unhesitatingly, whatever the danger involved. He should never show that he is afraid of danger or hard work, but on the contrary appear more relaxed. There is no safe place on the battlefield, and the more an upright man risks his life for his country, his king, and his honour, the more God is seemingly bound to protect him.

This is not to say that he should behave with reckless rashness, but that he should always remain in the post assigned to him and not go off on some individual exploit of his own.

If, as she hopes, he is promoted in due course, he must take care to familiarise himself with his new duties and responsibilities; and in this connection it will be very advantageous for him to make a study of fortification and of artillery.

He should treat all soldiers honourably and kindly, doing them all the little favours he can, but avoiding any excess, and dispensing his favours according to their merits.

Warfare inevitably involves bearing with numerous hardships, but he should never seem disheartened or depressed by them, nor complain of exhaustion, for only low-class and base people behave in this way. He should always appear resolute and cheerful; and so he will find the hardships less onerous, and in due course come to disregard them.

He must never boast of any exploit, but always speak of it modestly, giving the glory to God alone.

His father has presumably arranged for him to serve in the regiment commanded by the Marquis of Fontes, whose example he should carefully follow. He should do nothing without the prior advice or approval of the Marquis, and do his best to earn his favour.

He should not be fussy about what he eats, but accept gladly and gratefully whatever is given him. He should treat the servants of the Marquis kindly and well.

If he has any spare time, he should not fail to consult his books, 'because the study of letters does not interfere with the use of arms; but rather, he who is master of the former is a better wielder of the latter'. He should not be misled by the advice of ill-intentioned or ignorant people who try to persuade him that books are useless blunderbusses for a campaign, but he should realise that 'the sciences are good weapons for all emergencies'. Nor should he forget in the field what he has learnt with so much effort at home.

Lastly, he should remember that although he may be at a great distance from his father, reports of his good or ill conduct are bound to reach him. She therefore hopes that her son will behave in such wise that he will deserve many blessings from his parents, and that God will protect and guard him for many years.

Lisbon, 2 June 1704. 'Your very loving mother,
Countess of Assumar.'

GLOSSARY

Aldeia: Village. In Brazil, a mission-village; in Portuguese India, usually an Indian village paying rent or tribute to a Portuguese landlord, or the Crown, or the Church.

Alvará: Royal decree.

Audiencia: High Court. The highest tribunals of justice in Spanish America and the Philippines. They also had some extensive administrative functions.

Cabeça do casal: Legal head of a married couple, family, or household.

Casado: married man, usually a householder.

Conquistas: Conquests. The term most commonly used for the Portuguese overseas possessions, whether these had been acquired by force of arms or peacefully.

Conquistador: Conqueror.

Cruzado: Portuguese coin, originally of gold, whose value was fixed at 400 *reis* in 1517; later also of silver with the same nominal value, but of greatly differing intrinsic worth. During the seventeenth century the *cruzado* was roughly valued at four shillings (English), but in 1710 the English envoy at Lisbon equated it at 'about half a crown'.

Degredado: banished criminal; exiled convict.

Desembargador: High Court Judge; senior Crown lawyer in the Portuguese judiciary.

Donas de Zambesia: ladies of Zambesia; female *prazo*-holders.

Donatário: Lord-proprietor: landowner with some administrative and criminal jurisdiction.

Dote: Dowry.

Encomienda: A system under which Spanish conquerors, settlers, and their descendants collected tribute tax from Amerindians (and Filipinos) in certain specified areas, providing them in exchange with military protection and religious instruction. The application of the system varied widely at different times and in different places.

Estado da India: 'State of India'. Term loosely applied to all the Portuguese fortresses and settlements between the Cape of Good Hope and Japan.

135

Feitoria: Old English 'Factory'; trading agency or settlement, sometimes fortified.

Fidalgo: lit. Filho d'algo, 'son of somebody'; gentleman, nobleman. Portuguese equivalent of the Spanish *hidalgo.*

Flota: Fleet. Usually applied to the Spanish Treasure-Fleets.

Hidalgo: lit. Hijo d'algo, 'son of somebody'; gentleman; nobleman.

Jihad: Muslim Holy War against unbelievers.

Lavadeira: lit. 'washerwoman'. Applied to the resident coloured mistress of a white man in the island of São Tomé.

Limpeza de sangue (P), *Limpieza de sangre* (Sp): 'Purity of blood' from religious, racial and class standpoints. Muslim, Heretic, Black African and white working-class ancestry all being regarded as defiling or degrading in various degrees.

Mameluco: Brazilian mixed blood, usually the offspring of White father and Amerindian mother.

Manceba: mistress, concubine.

Mayorazgo: entailed estate; heir or occupant through primogeniture of entailed estate. Spanish equivalent of the Portuguese *morgado.*

Mestiço (P), *Mestizo* (Sp), Person of mixed blood. Often equated with a Mulatto in Africa and in Brazil, with a Eurasian in Asia, and with a Euro-Amerindian in Spanish America.

Morador: head of a household; citizen; settler.

Morgado: Entailed estate; also applied to the holder of one through primogeniture. Portuguese equivalent of the Spanish *mayorazgo.*

Mui-tsai: indentured Chinese child or teen-ager, usually a girl.

Oidor: High Court Judge, Circuit Judge, of the Spanish *Audiencia.*

Orfãas del Rei: Orphan girls of marriageable age sent from Portugal to the colonies (principally to Goa) to be married at the Crown's expense.

Ouvidor: High Court Judge, Circuit Judge of the Portuguese *Relação.*

Parda (f), Pardo (m): Person of colour; mixed blood, often with the connotation of Negro blood.

Pardao (pardau): Gold and silver coins struck in Portuguese India with a face value of 360 *reis* and 300 *reis* respectively. Also used for money of account.

Peça (Peça de Indias): Standard measure of classification for Negro slaves, according to age, sex and physical condition.

Poderosos: Powerful (influential) people, apt to abuse the superiority of their social status by oppressing their social inferiors.

Praça(s): Stronghold(s); term commonly applied to the fortified coastal towns in Morocco, West Africa, India, etc.

Prazero: Owner or occupant of a *prazo*, q.v.

Prazo: Estate in Zambesia, similar in some respects to a fief, but held on a mixture of European and African systems of tenure.

Prazo da Coroa: Crown *Prazo*, usually entailed in the female line from *c.* 1670.

Presidio: Garrison Town, such as Oran in Algeria and Melilla in Morocco.

Pundonor: Point of honour; sense of honour; nicety or scruple in honour.

Quilombo: Bantu War-camp in Angola. Community of runaway slaves in Brazil.

Raça (Raza) infecta: 'Contaminated Race', in practice applied chiefly to persons of Jewish or of Black Africa origins.

Recolhimento: Retirement House.

Regimento: Standing orders; set of instructions; rules and regulations.

Reinol (Reinóis): European-born Portuguese.

Reis (pl. of *Real*): Small Portuguese copper coin of low value which was abolished in the sixteenth century, but its multiples were retained for use as money of account.

Relação: Portuguese High Court of Justice. Roughly the equivalent of the Spanish *Audiencia*, but with far fewer administrative functions.

Roça: A sugar-plantation or large agricultural estate in São Tomé and Angola; in Brazil, more often applied to a small estate, a market-garden, or allotment.

Sertão: Backlands.

INDEX OF PERSONAL NAMES

BIBLIOGRAPHICAL INDEX

This index contains the names of authors or editors. The number after a name refers to the page where the author/editor's work is first mentioned and given a full citation (usually in a footnote). Where the entry is followed by two or more numbers, these refer to other works by the same person. A few titles are listed where a full citation has been inadvertently omitted in the text, or for the sake of clarification.